Dear Juniors,

This is a new expanded edition of the book that tells you how to handle your dog and how to compete in Junior Showmanship. There are lessons for you to follow and helpful hints to guide you.

You will learn how Junior Showmanship began and how it has changed. In the Junior Hall of Fame you will meet the champion handlers of Junior Showmanship over the years. How to begin a junior club and careers for junior graduates are discussed. You will find a place to keep your own records and notes. There is a special chapter for parents. For judges we have added the new chapter — How To Judge Junior Showmanship. Every subject is illustrated with photographs and drawings.

We hope that this book will help you become a better handler and a more knowledgeable dog fancier.

Your friends,
Marsha and Bethny

P.S. This is NEW!

The New Complete
JUNIOR SHOWMANSHIP HANDBOOK

This book belongs to

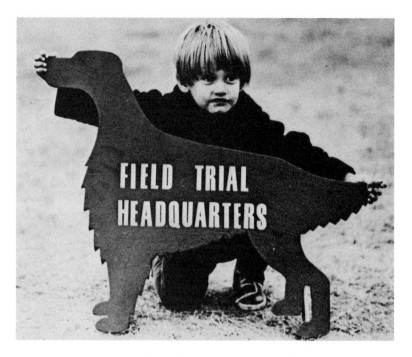

Too young to handle! *Photo courtesy R. Schepper*

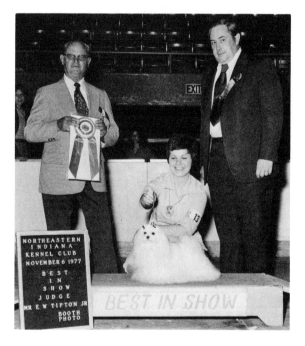

Former Junior Showman and now a professional handler, Daryl Martin is pictured above with Ch. Joanne-Chen's Mino Maya Dancer, the #1 Maltese in 1977. *Photo Martin Booth*

The New Complete
JUNIOR SHOWMANSHIP HANDBOOK

by
MARSHA HALL BROWN
BETHNY HALL MASON
Illustrated

A book of instruction on
HOW TO BEGIN
HOW TO HANDLE
and **HOW TO WIN**
in Junior Showmanship competition at dog shows
and
HOW TO JUDGE Junior Showmanship Classes

SECOND EDITION

HOWELL
BOOK HOUSE
New York

Howell Book House
Macmillan Publishing Company
866 Third Avenue, New York, NY 10022

Collier Macmillan Canada, Inc.
1200 Eglinton Avenue East, Suite 200
Don Mills, Ontario M3C 3N1

Library of Congress Cataloging in Publication Data

Brown, Marsha Hall.
    The new complete junior shownmanship handbook.

    First published in 1971 under title: The junior showmanship handbook.
    SUMMARY: Discusses the basics of showing dogs in junior showmanship classes, including background of the competition, AKC rules, skills required, how to prepare for shows, and profiles of outstanding winners.
    1. Dog shows—Junior showmanship classes.
(1. Dogs—Showing.   2. Dog shows)   I. Mason, Bethny Hall, joint author.   II. Title.
III. Title: Junior showmanship handbook.
SF425.13.B76   1980   636.7′08′88   79-25829
ISBN 0-87605-655-9

Macmillan books are available at special discounts for bulk purchases for sales promotions, premiums, fund-raising, or educational use. For details, contact:

                Special Sales Director
                Macmillan Publishing Company
                866 Third Avenue
                New York, NY 10022

10 9 8 7 6

Printed in the United States of America

To

THOMAS WATKINS HALL
and
FLORENCE FARRIER HALL

for *his* perseverance and dedication;
for *her* patience and understanding;
for *their* example of sportsmanship,
hard work and zest for living.

Contents

All drawings and hand-lettering in this book are by Bethny Mason

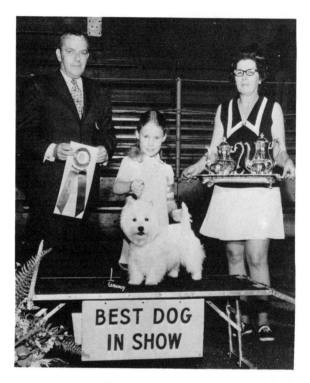

BEST DOG
IN SHOW

The youngest handler to ever score an all-breed Best in
Show in American Kennel Club history—Laura Mei-
sels, eight years old, of Houston, Texas. At the Cal-
casieu KC show at Lake Charles, La. on April 17, 1971,
Laura guided her West Highland White Terrier, White
Oaks Lover Boy, from the classes to win of the Group
under judge Maxwell Riddle, and on to the pictured
win of Best in Show under judge Vance H. Evans.
Entry was nearly 700 dogs. Laura finished Lover Boy to
championship in four shows. In her one time in Junior
Showmanship competition, at Houston in March 1971
before the present 10-year-old minimum was in effect,
Laura was Best Junior Handler in Show.

ACKNOWLEDGMENTS

TO Doug Belter, Susan Hutchinson, Bethny Brown, Mark Richardson, Jill Perkins, Rebecca Mason, Christine McFadden, Todd Pickton, Daryl Martin, and Stephen Osterling, Jr.—and to Topper, Persy, Tulip, Lucinda, Pzazz, Bunny, Kabou, Sam, Thorin, Happy, George and Nicky for their patience in front of our cameras.

The photographs taken exclusively for this book are by Sandy Schepper, Shay Pickton, Ray Mason and Bob Brown.

We appreciate the special contributions of Lydia Coleman Hutchinson and Karen Gard Spurlin.

Leonard Brumby, Jr., Mrs. William H. Long, Elsworth S. Howell, Thomas Yahn and the American Kennel Club made it possible for us to write the history of Junior Showmanship.

"You Can Be A Six-Star Junior" first appeared as an article in *Popular Dogs* by Marsha Hall Brown. Used with permission.

We thank, too, our families and friends for their help and support.

9

Above:
Marsha presenting the JS Hand book to Kenneth Mills, JS winner at Calgary, Alberta, Canada. *Hodges photo*

Left:
Bethny with Pell and Pym at Stone Gables. *Photo, Providence Journal Company*

Foreword

JUNIOR SHOWMANSHIP has advanced strongly in the nine years since the first edition of this Handbook appeared.

Much credit for its growth in the 1970's is due the American Kennel Club whose support wisely recognizes young fanciers of today as the breeders, exhibitors, judges, veterinarians and other dog authorities of tomorrow. Parents, dog club officers, professional handlers and other adults also share the honor in sponsoring this worthwhile, educational and character-building activity. And the Juniors themselves, by their dedication and diligence, represent the finest examples of sportsmanship in dogdom.

In their own youth the authors of this book, Marsha Hall Brown and Bethny Hall Mason, typified the all-American girl. The versatility of their interests and achievements was then—and is today—remarkable.

Marsha began showing dogs when she was only nine years old. In 1955 she won the Gaines Youth Award for Girl Show Dog Fancier of the Year. She handled many of her family's English Setters and other breeds to championships, Best of Breed and Sporting Group wins. She won ten first prizes in Children's Handling and Junior Showmanship.

A licensed all-breed handler for five years, she became a judge fourteen years ago and is currently approved for all Setters and JS. She has judged seven Setter specialty shows including those of the English Setter Association of America in 1973 and 1978.

For ten years Marsha wrote an outstanding column on JS for *Popular Dogs* Magazine and later became the English Setter columnist for the AKC's *The American Kennel Gazette*.

Mrs. Brown served as Vice President of the English Setter Association of America for five years and is a founding member of the Hudson English Setter Club. She has been a handling instructor, and her two daughters have also competed in JS.

Marsha has achieved much success in other fields. As a high school student, she was a member of the Rhode Island Honor Society and editor of its yearbook. Training in the National Red Cross Aquatic School, she became Director of Swimming and Water Safety for the town of Smithfield, R.I. Now in her 34th year of Girl Scouting, she was leader of Brownies, Juniors and Cadettes for twenty years. She has organized volunteers for the Red Cross Blood Donor Program, taught First Aid for Animals and presented a Pet Care Program for elementary schools.

Her sister, Bethny Hall Mason, also accomplished high honors in a variety of activities. In high school Bethny was President of the Girls Athletic Association, also a member of the Rhode Island Honor Society, and won the Spartan medal, an annual award to the writer of the best essay. Bethny was active in the Red Cross, particularly in its Aquatic School. She was swimming instructor for North Providence, R.I., and held the same position for the Girl Scouts of Rhode Island. She is a member of the Gloucester Historical Society and the Huguenot Society of Rhode Island. Her community efforts include Publicity Chairman for an elementary school executive board, membership in a Parent-Teacher League and presentation on dog care and careers related to dogs at elementary schools.

Bethny showed her first dog at a sanction match at the tender age of four years. When only 11, she finished her first champion and, in all, guided ten dogs to their AKC titles. In addition to English Setters, she handled Irish and Gordon Setters, Pointers, Afghans, Beagles and Schipperkes. She joined her sister as columnist for *Popular Dogs*. She is eligible to judge English Setters and JS. Her assignments have included the Governor's Foot Guard Show in Hartford, Ct., the Twin Brooks KC show in New Jersey, and the English Setter Specialty in New Jersey on February 13, 1977.

Bethny's record in Junior Showmanship may never be equalled. She won a total of 81 Firsts in the Open Class of that competition. For the years 1956, 1957, and 1958, she won the Stewards' Club of America award as the National Girl Show

12

Handler of the Year. For three consecutive years she was the Champion Junior Handler of both the English Setter Club of New England and the English Setter Association of America. In 1958 Governor Ribicoff of Connecticut presented her with the Best Junior Handler trophy awarded annually by that state's governor. In 1959 she duplicated her sister's achievement by winning the Gaines award as Girl Show Dog Fancier of the Year. Her record at the prestigious Westminster Kennel Club Junior Showmanship competition was incredible—in 1956 and 1957 she won third place at this event, and in 1959 won its top award, retiring from Junior Showmanship at only 13 years of age.

In this new edition, Marsha and Bethny have revised and greatly expanded the information and guidance presented in their first JS Handbook. They have added many new tips on how to handle and win and how to dress properly in today's styles. They have had many new photographs taken to show Juniors more clearly the steps to take in posing and gaiting their dogs in JS competition. The "Hall of Fame" chapter is updated to include the latest stars in JS with their pictures and winning records.

An entirely new chapter, "How to Judge Junior Showmanship," will be eagerly read by JS judges and others, including older Junior Showmen, who are contemplating application to the AKC for approval to judge this competition.

As the winner—in a class of two!—of the second Children's Handling Class held in America many years ago, I am delighted to present *The New Complete* JUNIOR SHOWMANSHIP HANDBOOK to young people, their parents and other supporters of this splendid competition.

—ELSWORTH HOWELL

Leonard Brumby, Sr.

George F. Foley

The founders of Junior Showmanship

14

1/The Story of
Junior Showmanship

IN the late 1920s, some active dog fanciers became interested in encouraging the participation of young people at the dog shows. These fanciers were mainly from the Long Island and Westchester areas of New York, and from southern Connecticut. They believed that the future of the dog world depended upon the interest and activities of the youth of the present.

Leonard Brumby, Sr., Founder

Leonard Brumby, Sr., was a well-known professional handler, and a member and officer of the Westbury Kennel Club. He worked hard to convince members and other exhibitors that it was important for children to take an active part in dog shows. Mr. Brumby felt that the children should have their own competition. He suggested that a competition based on handling ability would be particularly helpful and interesting for them. As a result of his efforts, the first Children's Handling Class was held at the Westbury Kennel Club show, Long Island, N.Y. in 1932.

Candy for All

The first classes for Children's Handling were listed in the Westbury premium list (the announcement that is sent out in advance of each show to let exhibitors know what prizes are being offered) as follows:
Class A—Boys under 14 years.
Class B—Girls under 14 years.

In 1933, the Westbury club offered Children's Handling for boys and girls under 15 years of age, and another class for boys and girls under 10 years of age. "Candy for all, but no unruly dogs," was announced in the premium list.

George F. Foley, who was superintendent of many of the large shows at the time, took an active interest in the Children's Handling classes. He encouraged the show-giving clubs to include a competition for young people. Soon there were Children's Handling classes at many of the dog shows in the East.

Westminster Competition

In 1933, the first Children's Handling Championship was held at the Westminster Kennel Club show at Madison Square Garden in New York City. Boys and girls who had won a first place in Children's Handling during the year were eligible to compete. However, juniors who scored three first place wins were barred from further competition until after the Westminster finals. The winner of the Handling Championship was presented with the Grand Challenge Trophy.

The Memorial Trophy

In 1949, the Professional Handlers' Association presented the Westminster Children's Handling Champion with a new trophy. The Leonard Brumby Sr. Memorial Trophy became the most famous junior award. Given in honor and memory of the founder of Children's Handling, the trophy is still awarded annually.

Changes and More Changes

The name of the competition was changed from Children's Handling to Junior Showmanship in 1951.

Children's Handling had begun with a handful of boys and girls in the New York area, and had grown to be a popular sport in which thousands of young people, throughout the United States and Canada, participated. What had originally been just a novel contest for children and their dogs became a highly competitive and sophisticated competition.

Changes developed in the selection of judges and in judging procedures. In the early years, there were no special qualifications required of Children's Handling judges. Celebrities and movie stars were often invited to judge, and their choice of a winner was not always based on skillful handling. Boys and girls were sometimes requested to exchange dogs with others in the class. The Professional Handlers Association acted to correct this situation by encouraging its members to judge more often, and soon only licensed handlers were allowed to preside.

There were changes in the class divisions, too. The Children's Handling classes were usually divided into a class for boys, and a class for girls. Large shows sometimes provided two classes for each, with an age division. Soon after the competition became Junior Showmanship, however, the classes were opened to either boys or girls, and divided by age only.

Further major changes were introduced in the mid-1950s. A class for novice juniors was offered, and experienced juniors were provided with open competition. As the popularity of Junior Showmanship grew, these Novice and Open classes were divided by age.

In 1971 Junior Showmanship achieved full status. The American Kennel Club announced its official recognition of the competition. Rules and regulations were standardized. Licensed professional handlers and eligible breed judges were chosen to judge the competitions. In 1974 the AKC invited former Juniors to apply for Junior Showmanship Judging eligibility. With the end of formal licensing of professional handlers in 1977, the AKC approved as judges for JS only breed judges and Junior Showmanship judges.

2/How to Begin in Junior Showmanship

HI! Welcome to the world of Junior Showmanship. Beginning this new adventure with your dog will be fun. It will be interesting. It will be exciting. You will meet many interesting people and you will make new friends. So, let's not wait any longer—let's begin.

Be An Observer

Go to several shows as a visitor. Watch the competition in the breed you will be handling.

Notice that each class that enters the ring is judged in a similar way. The judge motions for all dogs to trot (or gait) around the ring. He then examines each dog individually. First he examines the dog in a standing or show pose position. Then he watches the dog in motion. After he has judged all the dogs in the ring and made his decision, he sends the chosen dogs to the place markers in the ring and awards the ribbons to the handlers.

Observe the people who are handling in the ring. How do they gait the dog? How do they pose the dog? How do they handle the lead? (In dog shows, the leash is usually called the lead—you lead your dog into the ring. In this book, we will use the word *lead*.)

Now go to the Junior Showmanship ring and watch the classes carefully. Note that the fine points of the dog are not being considered here. THE JUNIORS ARE JUDGED ONLY ON THEIR ABILITY TO HANDLE. Because it is handling abilities rather than dogs that are being judged, the Junior Showmanship classes often take longer to judge.

The three basic handling skills will be required for Junior Showmanship: juniors will gait their dogs together around the ring, will pose their dogs for examination, and will gait their dogs individually. Juniors are also tested on other handling skills, such as gaiting in a certain pattern, posing the dog in a line parallel (side by side) to other dogs, or being required with another junior to gait their dogs at the same time.

Learn the Rules

Look in the show catalog for the rules and classes offered for Junior Showmanship at the show. Age requirements and the number and type of classes may differ at shows. Most shows use the following competition announcement:

Novice Junior: For boys and girls who are at least ten years old and under 13 years old on the day of the show and who, at the time entries close have not won three (3) first place awards in a Novice Class.

Novice Senior: For boys and girls who are at least 13 years old and under 17 years old on the day of the show and who at the time entries close have not won three (3) first place awards in a Novice Class.

Open Junior: For boys and girls who are at least ten years old and under 13 years old on the day of the show and who have won three (3) first place awards in a Novice JS Class.

Open Senior: For boys and girls who are at least 13 years old and under 17 years old on the day of the show and who have won three (3) first place awards in a Novice JS Class.

Best Junior Handler: The first place winners in each of the classes, if undefeated in any other JS class at that show, shall be eligible to compete.

Each dog handled in a regular Junior Showmanship class must be entered and shown in one of the breed or Obedience classes at the show, or must be entered for Junior Showmanship only. Each dog must be owned or co-owned by the junior handler, or by the junior handler's father, mother, brother, sister, uncle, aunt, grandfather or grandmother, including the corresponding step and half relations. Every dog entered for Junior Showmanship must be eligible to compete in dog shows or Obedience trials. At a specialty show, each dog must be of the breed for which the show is held.

A dog that has been excused or disqualified by a breed judge or by a Bench Show Committee may still be handled in Junior Showmanship if eligible to compete in Obedience trials. However, a dog that has been rejected, dismissed or excused by the veterinarian for the protection of the other dogs at the show, or for the protection of the dog excused, may not be handled in Junior Showmanship.

Prizes shall be awarded for skillful handling only, merit of the dog not to count.

Eight or more First Place wins in the Open Divisions are required to compete for the Leonard Brumby, Sr. Memorial Trophy each year at the Westminster Kennel Club show, Madison Square Garden, N.Y. in February.

A Helping Hand

Seek the help of someone who handles your breed and knows the correct ways to pose and gait this breed.

The breed association or club may have a member in charge of junior activities or they may suggest a member who will help you. A breeder who handles and is familiar with proper handling skills may be helpful. A professional handler who has had experience with your breed may also be helpful. Remember: each breed is handled in a particular way. It is necessary that you learn the proper way to handle your breed.

Ready, Set, Handle!

Now it is time to take the lead in your hand. At home, find a place to practice. This can be in your yard, at a nearby park, or an unused area of a parking lot or school yard. In winter weather your practice space may be a garage or basement. If possible, set up a practice ring with five stakes and twine or yarn. Or use five bricks or similar objects to mark off the area you will use for a temporary ring. Chalk can also be used to mark a temporary ring on pavement.

Exercise your dog for several minutes before you begin the practice session. It is important that your dog be comfortable and calm before each lesson.

Now place the show lead on your dog. If your dog is properly shown on a tight lead, place the lead high on the neck and under the throat so that you have complete control of the dog.

Hold the lead in your left hand. Extend your left arm out from your shoulder so that your arm is parallel to the ground. Your elbow should be slightly bent. Gather all the extra lead inside your hand. Secure your grasp on the lead by looping the first inch of lead next to your hand, over your index finger and under your remaining fingers.

If your dog is properly shown on a loose lead, place the lead high on the neck. Hold the lead in your left hand. Support the dog's head with your right hand. Pull the lead gently under the ear and forward. Take your first step and pull the lead further forward. Drop your right hand. Let out enough lead so that your dog has space to move. Gather all the extra lead inside your hand. Secure your grasp on the lead by looping the first inch of the lead next to your hand over your index finger and under your remaining fingers. Caution: Your dog must be trained to move properly on a loose lead. Make sure you can control your dog.

Enter the practice ring with your dog on your left and the show lead in your left hand. Turn right and walk all the way around the inside of the ring. **Ring traffic always travels counter-clockwise.** Now that you know the route, go around the ring again. Move at a speed which allows your dog to trot easily at your side.

Bring your dog to a stop. Place your dog in a show pose. Remember how the dogs looked at the show in the breed class? Remember how the handlers carefully placed the feet and held the dog in a pose? Is your dog posed correctly for its breed? Are you holding the head and tail or lead and tail in the proper way? Do you have control over your dog?

Get ready to gait. Place the lead high on the neck and hold the lead in the left hand. Begin at one side of the ring and walk in a straight line across the ring and STOP.

Do not move from your gaiting position. Is your left arm extended shoulder height? Is your dog on your left?

Extend your free hand (right hand) across in front of you and reach for your left hand. (Do not move your body or feet.) Transfer the lead coil from your left hand into your right hand. Place your left hand at your side and turn toward that hand until you are facing the direction of return. Walk back across the ring in a straight line.

This time, your dog will be on your right side. Your right arm is extended out and you are holding the lead in your right hand. Now repeat this straight-line gaiting exercise several times moving your dog at the proper speed.

There are two proper ways to change direction without changing hands:

1. Walk across the ring in a straight line with your dog on your left. With your left arm extended, turn your dog to the right in a semi-circle around you. Pivot on your right foot

and turn to your right until you and your dog are facing the direction of return.

2. Walk across the ring in a straight line with your dog on your left. Turn your dog to the left in a semi-circle. Use longer strides to keep yourself next to your dog until you are both facing the direction of return. Practice both of these straight-line gaiting exercises. Find out which one is correct for the breed you handle.

You have now performed the three basic handling skills: gaiting in a circle, posing your dog, and gaiting in a straight line. You have also learned how to enter the ring, how to hold the lead securely, and how to change hands and direction.

Make this fun for your dog. Keep this practice session short. Plan ten minutes for the adult dog and half that time for a puppy. Regular daily practice is important for you and your dog. Two long sessions twice a week should not be substituted for daily practice. Praise your dog often at practice time. Reward your dog at the end of each session with a cheerful voice and a short playtime. Remember: learn to control, train and handle your dog, but do it with a gentle hand and a kind heart.

Sanctioned matches are for you. A match is a practice show which is sanctioned by the American Kennel Club. Many breed clubs and all-breed clubs hold these informal shows during the year. Most matches offer breed, Obedience and Junior Showmanship classes. If possible make your debut at a local match show. You may get extra practice there by handling your dog in in the breed classes, as well as in Junior Showmanship.

Your first competition in Junior Showmanship is a big adventure. Whether it is at a match show or a regular point show (in which championship points are awarded) three helpful hints will speed you to early success:

1. Watch the other Junior Showmanship Classes.
2. When the judge is through, ask for corrective criticism.
3. Remember your dog—pat him and praise him. You couldn't have competed without him.

3/How to Look
Like A Winner

YOUR whole appearance is just as important as the way you handle. Your clothes, grooming and manners can make you look like a winner. Always be well groomed. Choose clothes which are appropriate for a sporting event and comfortable to work in. Make sure they are clean, neat, and pressed.

Be courteous to the judge and to other handlers. Be especially considerate toward juniors who are just beginning. Be a good sport. Congratulate the winner before you leave the ring. Don't get upset if you are not the judge's choice today.

Leave your emotions at home.

For Boys

The winning look for boys should include a jacket and tie. Either a suit or sport jacket with slacks is recommended. Jacket and turtleneck, shirt with tie and vest, or leisure suits are acceptable. Notice that the most successful handlers are well-dressed with jacket and tie, even in hottest weather.

Wear well-tailored sport clothes. Don't choose the lates fad or the loudest print. The wrong clothes are apt to draw attention to you and away from your dog. Plain styles and subtle colors or prints are best. Choose a color that contrasts with the color of your dog. Don't wear anything uncomfortable or tight. Keep your jacket buttoned or it will interfere with your handling. Do wear a tie clip. Clothes should be amply cut to allow freedom of movement.

Put your best foot forward in comfortable shoes. Soft rubber soles are noiseless and they give you secure footing on slippery floors. A soft flexible shoe with good support and thick soles is best for handling. Do not wear boots or sandals.

Don't forget a practical hair cut. Hair falling down in your eyes will distract your every move. Is your dog better trimmed than you are?

For Girls

The winning look for girls has a greater variety. Skirt and blouse, skirt and sweater, suit, jumper, culottes, gauchos, dress or pant suit are all acceptable. Slacks should be worn. only when they are part of a pants suit with either matching vest or jacket. Never wear jeans or shorts. The color, style and material should be attractive on you and be in contrast to your dog. (Example: if you are handling a black Poodle, wear a light colored dress such as yellow or tan to give a good background for your dog.)

Choose a plain tailored look and you cannot go wrong. Some suggestions are: a stitched-down pleated skirt and blazer jacket, an A-line jumper dress (pockets, please) or a sport suit with pleated or A-line skirt. These will be comfortable, fit better, and stay neat-looking longer. You will always look fresh in permanent press fabrics. They are now common in winter and summer weight fashions and many are stain and wrinkle resistant. Save the latest fad for school wear. Don't wear your skirts too short or too long. Remember you must be free to bend, kneel, and run gracefully. Long full skirts or dresses will interfere with your handling and may hide your dog. Don't wear a design or print that will detract from your dog. Don't wear jewelry that will bother your dog or other handlers' dogs. Too many bracelets that jangle are a nuisance.

Check yourself in a mirror at home. Assume the different handling positions and see if your choice of clothes is correct.

Think ahead. Your hairdo should be youthful (10–17), neat, and secure. Your hair should never be in your way while you are handling. Style your hair so that your "lovely locks" cannot fall or blow in your face, or in your line of vision, or become a bother to you in any way.

Make-up for juniors over thirteen should be natural looking. Please keep cosmetics to a minimum and do not use eye make-up.

Tie or buckle shoes with soft comfortable soles are the best. No heels, boots, or sandals, please. Wear either stockings or knee socks. Make sure your stockings are free from runs. Carry a spare pair just in case.

Important—things to have in a emergency:
  Do you have comb or hair brush?
  Clothes brush?
  Spot remover?
  Raincoat you can handle in?
  Needle and thread and safety pin?
  An extra handkerchief?
  Extra shoes or tennis shoes?
  Extra pair of stockings?

Now that you look like a winner from head to foot, go in the ring and be a winner!

When your dog will not
stand for the posing
And he moves 'cross the
ring with a grudge
Just remember the Rule
that is Golden
Keep The Dog Between
You And The Judge

4/How to Handle in Junior Showmanship

THIS chapter explains junior competition, the "golden rules of Junior Showmanship" and the ideal Junior Showman. It also includes the treasures of this book . . . six complete handling lessons. To find out how much you have learned, take the test at the end of the chapter.

Junior Showmanship is a competition in which young people are judged on their ability to handle a dog. The prime objective for the junior competitor is to demonstrate his or her ability in showing the dog to its best advantage. Throughout the various ring procedures and examinations, the junior competitor must strive to make his or her dog the most appealing. The points of the dog do not count. The junior must demonstrate that he or she knows the dog's faults and has learned how to minimize them.

Junior competitors must practice the golden rule of JS— **keep the dog between you and the judge.** Whether handling the dog in a show pose or handling the dog in motion, the junior must always keep the dog in full view of the judge.

The ideal Junior Showman must love dogs and enjoy handling them.

The ideal Junior Showman must be business-like in manner and appearance.

The ideal Junior Showman must practice regularly, seek corrective criticism and try to improve all handling skills.

The ideal Junior Showman must study the breed he handles and be knowledgeable of his own dog's conformation.

The ideal Junior Showman must be honest, courteous and considerate.

On the Move

STEP 1: How to Walk, How to Run

Toddlers have learned to walk and are just learning how to run. Did you know many juniors have to learn these motions all over again? When you walk to school or run for the bus, your body is in balance and your arms are free. When you handle a dog, your body is slightly turned, your head and neck are turned, and one arm and hand are at work. Therefore, you must adapt to this different position when you handle your dog in motion.

Now, let's begin. Take the lead in your left hand and extend your left arm at shoulder level. Correct your posture by raising the very top of your head to maximum height.

Look straight ahead and walk across the practice ring. Repeat this exercise taking BIG steps and quickening the pace. Always use a good long stride and adjust your speed to your dog's proper gait.

Practice walking several more times and check two problem areas:

(1) Your free arm should be at your side slightly swinging in coordination with your motion. If you have trouble keeping it down either practice swinging it slightly across in front of you by bending your elbow or place your hand in a make believe pocket at your side.

(2) Your head should always remain erect to insure proper posture. When you look at your dog, be sure you turn your head to the side and look slightly back over your shoulder.

Practice the walking exercise until it is correct and natural to you.

Look slightly back over your shoulder to check your dog.

Run with a strong straight forward stride.

Adjust your speed to your dog's proper gait.

Ready to run? All the positions you have just learned in walking are employed in running. The most important feature in this exercise is the size or length of your stride. Take the longest running step you can, and adjust your speed to your dog's proper gait. Your stride should be strong, straight forward and consistent. Correct and eliminate any bad habits such as running on your toes, leaping in mid-stride or bending your knees more than necessary. You should flex your knees enough for graceful efficient motion. Your knee should never be raised in front of you, nor should it be bent in back of you.

Remember: just because you are running, your posture should not change. If you handle a dog on a loose lead, you must be even more careful to run in an erect position.

Shorten lead for con-
trol to stop or turn.

Perfect posture and coordination between handler and dog.

STEP 2: Approach to the judge

There are three main reasons for the approach: to keep the dog in full view of the judge when turning to gait, to present your dog courteously for motion evaluation, and to get your dog started in motion before gaiting is examined.

From the right side of the ring, get ready to approach the judge who is in the top center of the ring. See diagram.

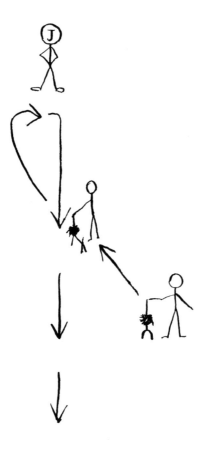

Face in the direction of the judge with your dog at your left side and the lead in your left hand. Walk out to the center of the ring slightly past the judge and turn your dog slowly toward the judge and in a semi-circle in front of the judge. Be sure you keep your handling arm at shoulder height on the turn so that the dog is "heads up" and ready to move.

roach to the judge.

Turn in a smooth semi-circle.

Move straight away with the dog directly in front of the judge.

Now check your position and your dog's position; your backs are to the judge. The lead is still in your left hand. The dog (not you) is directly in front of the judge. The dog is on your left side. Walk across the ring in a straight line. Make a proper change of direction turn and return to the judge. Repeat this exercise without stopping at any point.

The whole idea of the approach is to keep the dog in view and in motion. This exercise should be smooth and effortless. The judge should never have to move to watch your dog gait.

Now try the approach from the left side of the ring. Face toward the judge with your dog on your left and lead in your left hand. Walk out toward the judge. Turn your dog to the right in a semi-circle. Leave the judge with the lead in your left hand, the dog on your left side. Make sure that your dog is directly in line with the judge.

There are two problem areas in this exercise: (1) When you approach the judge and he stops you to give directions, stop leaving enough room to make a proper approach. Listen carefully to the directions and make sure you understand the requested gaiting pattern. Then make the approach. This is difficult and takes practice to look smooth. (2) When you return to the judge and he asks you to gait your dog again, keep your dog in motion by turning in a semi-circle in front of the judge. Do not change hands.

Note: In recent years there has been a trend toward a more natural style of handling. The value of moving a dog on a loose lead has been recognized by many. Hard and fast rules on changing lead hands have been modified. **The continued smooth motion of the dog without distracting movements of the handler is the most important goal.**

STEP 3: Gaiting patterns.

There are five main gaiting patterns which judges use to examine the moving dog. Junior handlers must be prepared to follow directions and move their dogs in the requested pattern. Let's begin by walking through the **I, L, T, O and the triangle.**

The "I" Pattern

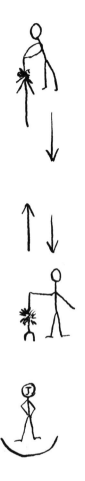

The "I" is simply down the ring and back in a straight line. There are three correct ways to execute the I pattern. Choose the proper pattern for your breed.

The "L" Pattern

For "L", walk down the ring in a straight line with your dog on your left side. Turn to the left and walk to the corner. Change hands so that the dog is in the judge's view and walk back to the point opposite the judge. Turn without changing hands and return in a straight line to the judge.

The "T" Pattern

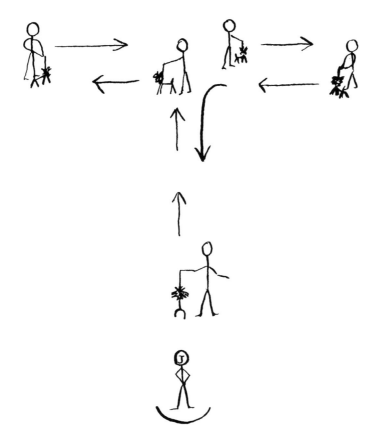

The "T" pattern is very similar to the "L". With the lead in your left hand, walk across the ring. Turn left and walk to the corner. Stop, change hands. Now walk all the way across the end of the ring. Stop, change hands, and return to the point opposite the judge. Return in a straight line to the judge.

The "O" Pattern

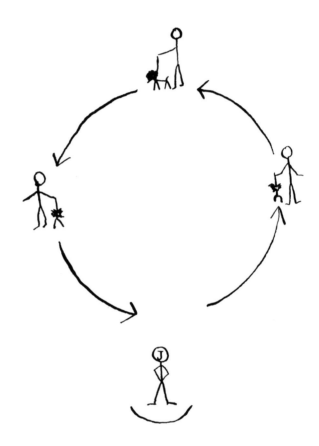

For the "O", hold the leash in your left hand and walk in a complete circle around the ring. This pattern is for individual gaiting and should be done in a circle somewhat smaller than the pattern used for all the dogs gaiting around the ring together.

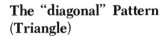

The "diagonal" Pattern
(Triangle)

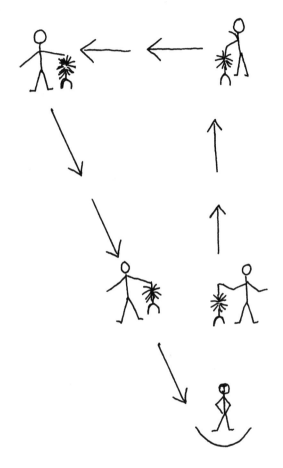

The "Triangle" pattern is similar to the L pattern. Walk down the ring in a straight line with your dog on your left side. Turn to the left and walk to the corner. From the corner continue in a straight line directly to the judge.

Keep dogs under control and gait at same speed.

There is one gaiting exercise which is not a pattern. When two dogs are asked to gait together the handlers are always positioned on the outside of the dogs and the dogs are side by side. Practice this with another person and try to keep the dogs together.

Now that you know what the gaiting patterns are, practice them at your normal speed. Begin with an approach each time.

**Review Steps One, Two and Three
with your dog "on the move."**

Position Is Everything

STEP 4: Setting up your dog.

This lesson starts with homework for you. First you must learn how the breed you handle is correctly posed. Study photographs of ideal specimens and pay particular attention to placement of legs, top line, posture of neck and head, and position of tail. Now observe how the expert handlers pose their dogs to look like the ideal specimens.

Study your own dog. Find out what your dog's good points are and learn how to show them. Know your dog's faults and learn how to disguise them.

Finished your homework? Let's practice. Walk into the practice ring and slowly bring your dog to a stop.

The control of your dog is the basis for every move you make in posing your dog. One hand is always used for control. If you pose your dog without a lead, your control hand will be holding the dog's head or muzzle. If your dog is shown on a lead, your control hand will be holding the short length of the lead.

Your dog is at your left side and the lead is in your left hand. If it applies to your breed, remove the lead slowly and place it near your right foot. As you turn to the side of your dog, change control to your right hand. In the following order, set your dog in the proper pose:

Place the dog's left front foot in position with your left hand.
Change control, to your left hand.
Place the dog's right front foot in position with your right hand.
Change control to your right hand.
Reach under your dog and place the left rear foot.
Place the right rear foot.
Check all four feet (in case your dog has moved.) Kneel on your left knee only. Control remains in your right hand.

Proper setting of front.

Alternate method of setting front.

Proper setting of rear.

Proper setting of rear.

Keep space between you and dog.

Knee closest to dog's head is always elevated.

Always keep your feet on the ground.

Your left hand is used to position the tail. (If this is not appropriate for your breed, your left hand should be at your side.) Make sure your control is skillful. Check the length of lead. It should not be too long or too short. Check the way you hold the muzzle. Your hand should not be in the judge's view.

Remember: this step applies to most breeds but there are exceptions. That is why you must do your homework at the beginning of this lesson. Some breeds are correctly set up by "dropping" them into position. Some breeds are correctly posed by maneuvering the dog into a natural position. Toys are posed with the handler kneeling. Large breeds are posed with the handler in a standing position. In the next chapter you will learn more about the handling of individual breeds.

Present the head. Make first impressions count.

STEP 5: The judge's examination

There are two parts to the judge's examination. First, the judge will examine your dog by touching and feeling major parts of the dog's anatomy. Second, the judge will step back and view your dog as a whole. You must be ready for both types of examination.

Get your dog ready. Let's begin. Walk into the practice ring with the lead in your left hand and bring your dog to a stop at the side of the ring. Pose your dog facing the line of direction and make sure you are in the proper position and posture. Get ready for the judge to approach. (During your practice sessions it is helpful to have someone "play" the part of the judge.) Your right hand is your control hand. When the judge approaches make sure that your hand is not limiting the view of your dog's face and head. When the judge begins to examine the dog's

49

Hold the tail. Place your thumb at the area below and to the side of the tail, to prevent the dog from moving.

head, pause to see if you are requested to show the dog's bite. Rise slowly with your back straight and move to the rear of your dog. If you pose your dog on a lead you may need to lengthen it for this position. Keep the lead taut for full control. While you are at the rear of the dog make sure the rear feet and legs are in position and hold the tail appropriately. It is also helpful to place your thumb at the area below and to the side of the dog's tail to prevent the dog from moving back during examination. If you are handling a very small breed it will be necessary for you to be in a squatting position at this time. Do not kneel. Do keep your back straight.

As the judge moves to the left side of your dog to examine the body, be ready to take the dog's head in your right hand and return to the dog's right side. Keep as far away from your dog as your arm length permits so that the judge has plenty of room and a clear view of the dog.

As the judge gets near the dog's hindquarters move slowly to the head and stand directly in front of your dog with both hands used for control. If you pose your dog on a lead, one

Stand at the dog's head. Keep
your feet apart. Bend from the waist.

With a large dog, *stand* at the rear.

hand is proper control. Check the dog's front feet and legs and be ready to move.

As soon as the judge completes the examination return to your dog's right side. Quickly check all four feet and pose your dog. Your posture should be correct here. Your head should be very slightly turned and your eyes should be toward your dog's head. Do not look up at the judge. Now relax your dog and pat him.

Practice this lesson several times. Then practice the examination routine beginning with your dog on the other side.

The most difficult part of this lesson is timing: when to be ready, when to move, when to make your dog look alert. As you practice, think about every move you make. Is it smooth? Is it correct? When you are handling at a show, pay attention to what is going on in the ring. Know where the judge is at all times. Be ready. Be alert.

Use both hands for control during examination.

A small junior with a large dog must use extended arms and legs to move smoothly around the dog.

STEP 6: How you and your dog can relax in the ring.

Most Junior Showmanship classes are large and it takes a long time to complete the judging. So you must practice ways to save your energy and your dog's energy and patience. The judge cannot look at you and your dog all the time, so learn to plan when it is possible to relax.

If there are a number of dogs in front of you and the judge has begun his examination, you can relax. But keep your eye on the judge. When the judge is almost ready to examine the dog in front of you, get in position and pose your dog. After the judge is at least two dogs behind you, relax again. While the judge is watching other juniors gait their dogs, you may relax until the dog before you is called out. At that time pose your dog so he looks his best, but have the lead on and be ready to move.

Important: "relax" in Junior Showmanship is not rest time for you and your dog. For you, it is a time to relax the muscles you use when posing your dog. For your dog, it is a stand-at-ease or occasionally a turn-around in place.

Take your dog into the practice ring and set him in a show pose. Now relax by standing at your dog's head. Pat your dog, and speak to him softly. If the weather is hot and the ring is in the sun, try to stand so that you cast a shadow over the dog's head. In hot weather let your dog relax with mouth open. Practice turning your dog around you. This will give your dog a rest from constant posing. However, be careful not to disturb others near you. Do not let your dog sit or lie down in the ring. Your attention must be on your dog and the judge at all times.

The Wide Stride—A Review

Now that you have completed the Six Steps of handling you are ready for the Wide Stride! This is a quiz to find out what skills you must spend more time on. After you have taken your Wide Stride quiz, check the list of tips at the end of this chapter.

Questions:
1. Set your dog in the proper pose. What must you do before you assume the proper position at the dog's side?
2. What is the first thing you must do when the judge approaches to examine your dog?
3. When two dogs are gaiting together the handlers should be on the _____ ?
4. How can you check your own posture?
5. After you have made the approach to the judge, the _____ should be directly in line with the judge.
6. Which of the three ways should you choose to do the I pattern?

Answers:
1. Check your dog's four feet.
2. Make sure that your hand is not limiting the view of your dog's face and head.
3. Outside.
4. Raise the very top of your head as high as possible.
5. Dog.
6. The way which is proper for your breed.

Remember: your final test is competing in Junior Showmanship. Study and practice are necessary for all handlers but there is no substitute for actual handling experience.

Special Tips

Work slowly, keep calm, don't rush.

Be methodical. Don't fuss and overwork. Don't make unnecessary motions.

Check your own position.

Always keep your back straight.

Use your extended arms to keep a space between you and your dog.

Use your hands in a firm grip but also use your hands to be kind and reassuring to your dog.

Use your legs for raising and lowering yourself so that you can always keep your back straight.

Always know where the judge is.

Be ready for the judge's examination.

Be courteous to others in the ring.

Keep a space between you and the person in front of you.

Don't crowd.

Use a squeaker (for certain breeds which should look alert) only when the judge is looking at your dog. It can be very distracting to other dogs.

Leave the dog's brush in the tack box.

Leave enough room between you and the dog in front to allow for handling and judging.

5/How to Win
in Junior Showmanship

IF it's worth doing, then it's worth doing well. This chapter explains how you can become a Junior Showmanship winner. You will find out how to really look at yourself and how to correct your mistakes. You will learn about the importance of your dog in competition, and how to make sure you have that special knowledge about the breed you handle.

Perfect Your Skills

There must be a reason for every move you make. Your dog's left foot is out of place? Fix it. Know exactly where to place the foot and then leave it alone. You have a reason to make these moves. Can you give a reason for all the moves you make? Are they necessary? Your eagerness and excitement can make you do things which are unnecessary. These moves can be distracting to your dog and can detract from his performance.

Make every move count. Know your dog well and have your dog fully prepared for Junior Showmanship competition.

Every move you make in the ring must benefit the dog you handle. Your moves can make the dog look better, behave better, and feel better. For example: the judge approaches your posed Collie. You know that you must be near the dog's head with proper hand controlling the lead. But how can you make this move really count? Fill this pause at the head with your skill as a handler. Get your Collie "on alert." Present to the judge a view of a devoted Collie watchful and waiting for a command.

Be proud of your accomplishment, be proud of your dog. Jennifer A. Sheldon, Westminster Kennel Club 1965 Junior Showmanship Winner, with her Afghan, Ch. Khabira Shady Lady.

Fortune Favors the Bold

Your attitude toward competing and handling can help make you a winner. It is essential that you enter the ring with a positive outlook. Say to yourself, "I can handle and I want to win." Too many juniors have the mistaken idea that handling to win has something to do with poor sportsmanship. They are defeated before they begin.

Handling to win is the attitude of the experienced and honest competitor. Sportsmanship is how you play the game and how you cope with winning and losing. Remember: you have come a long way as a junior handler and you have learned a great deal. Be proud of your accomplishment. Be proud of your dog. Have confidence in your own ability. Now go in the ring and win!

Apply Polish Where Needed

Your trophies will always be valuable, but they will only look their best when you keep them polished. To be a Junior Showmanship winner, you need polish, too. Polish every handling

57

skill and every motion you make. Pay particular attention to your posture, balance and gracefulness. Discipline yourself to be smooth in handling your posed dog. If you make believe you are in a slow motion film, your handling speed will be correct. Plan your gaiting and turns before the judge calls you out. Remember: the ideal handler uses all necessary skills to put the dog in the spotlight and himself out of notice.

Take a Good Look at Yourself

There are things you do and moves you make that you may not be aware of. Some are handling faults. Some are awkward motions. Some are unconscious gestures.

There are three ways to face your faults:

The best is to have a coach who can watch you at practice sessions and spot your errors. Your coach does not have to be experienced in dogs. It can be someone learning along with you. A parent or friend can follow the handling lessons and tips in this book and find your mistakes for you. Your coach should also watch you when you handle in competition to catch the mistakes you make at a real show.

Professional and amateur handlers who are experienced and knowledgeable in your breed can also be helpful. Ask them for corrective criticisms. Discuss with them the special skills used in handling your breed.

The use of home movies and a large practice mirror will allow you to actually see for yourself. If you have someone film your handling, make sure it includes both practice and competition. A large mirror on the kennel or garage wall will be a great aid when you and your dog must practice alone.

For You and Your Coach

There are a number of mistakes common to most learning handlers. Do they apply to you?

When you are rising from a kneeling position, keep your hands off your dog's back. Don't brace your elbow on your knee while holding your dog's head.

Get rid of the dog brush, while you are in the ring.

To bait is to tempt your dog with morsels. It should never become a display of dog feeding. Also, make sure that it is appropriate to use bait when handling your own breed. If you must bait, keep your actions between you and your dog.

If you use keys or a similar object to alert your dog, do it in a discreet manner. The only reason for baiting or alerting should be the reaction you get from your dog. Again, make sure this procedure is proper in your breed.

Important: the experts you watch do not always demonstrate proper handling. Be sure the skill is correct before you adopt it as your own. Handlers in the breed ring many times change a skill because of the dog they are handling. For example: a particular dog moves better on the right, so the handler keeps the dog on the right in the gaiting patterns.

You must also be sure not to copy a handler's individual mannerisms. There are three common examples of this. When you are kneeling with your dog posed, keep your back straight, head erect and your face turned slightly in the direction of your dog's head. Do not bend your neck or tip your head at some unnatural angle because you see someone else do it. Use a strong, confident, long stride when you run and do not flex your knees any more than necessary. It is unnaturally and physically tiring to bend your whole leg in two. Girls should be confident, athletic and in control—but also ladylike.

Now for personal problem areas. If you wear glasses make sure they are secure and do not slip. Use an elastic band if you wish. Many people who wear glasses have a habit of constantly pushing them back in place or making facial contortions because of the slipping. A handler can't spare his hands for fixing his glasses nor should he be "making faces" to prevent the slipping.

If your hair is distracting in any way, check this problem immediately.

Nervousness and excitement may affect your manners. Don't carry a fixed grin on your face while you're handling, and don't chatter (even to your dog) while the judge is examining it.

Doing What Comes Naturally

Practice and experience equal good handling. You have learned how to handle, how to improve your skills, how to correct your mistakes, and how to eliminate needless gestures. You should be an able handler now. You should be ready to carry out your perfected skills every time you handle. Good handling should be doing what comes naturally.

There is still room for improvement. Your sense of timing in all the things you do will improve with additional experience. You will also gain more poise as you compete. You should be handling well every time you compete. You should have a mature outlook and refrain from making excuses for poor performance.

Is Your Dog An Asset?

"The points of the dog not to count," says the Junior Showmanship rule. But now that you are an accomplished handler and are ready for top Junior Showmanship competition, you must take a good look at your partner. The best dog for Junior Showmanship does not have to be a great example of its breed. However, there are some important requirements.

Your dog must be a specimen of at least average quality. Intelligence, patience and good spirit are necessary. Your dog must be intelligent enough to respond to training, patient enough to endure the long Junior Showmanship classes and have sufficient spirit to move willingly at all times.

Your dog can help you win. If your dog is eye-catching, attention will be drawn to you. If your dog responds well to your handling, you will appear skillful and capable.

Your dog may also limit your success. An unruly or impatient dog will not provide the handler with the opportunity to demonstrate handling skills. A sluggish dog will only draw unfavorable attention to the handler. If the dog does not behave or respond properly to the handler, its action shows that little preparation has been made at home.

One of our personal anecdotes may help you understand the value of a good Junior Showmanship dog. Rellim was a big good-natured Setter. He was not the finest example of his breed but he was very attractive, carried a lovely coat, and had a fun-loving manner. Bethny trained him and practiced with him daily. He knew exactly what she expected of him and never let her down. However, Junior Showmanship judges became critical and said that the big Setter was so easy to handle that Bethny had very little to do to show him. Bethny solved that problem by tickling Rellim occasionally to make him move a foot. And, of course, she continued to win under the critical judges.

Remember: it's a team that competes in Junior Showmanship. You and your dog must know each other, like each other and work well together. The noted professional handler, Art Baines, once told us, "Show that dog 'til the ribbons are given out. Don't ever give up."

That Special Knowledge

To achieve excellence in handling you must know the background of the breed you handle so that you can present the dog in characteristic form and mood. It is a mistake to get between the judge and your dog. It is just as big an error to handle a Terrier in the same way as a Sporting Dog. Each breed is presented in a different way. For example: there is a difference in spirit and structure between the English Setter and the Irish Setter. Therefore, there are handling differences in these two breeds.

Are you ready to specialize your handling skills? You will find special handling tips on certain individual breeds at the end of this chapter. These tips also apply to similar breeds. Before you begin, make sure your dog is trimmed and groomed appropriately for its breed. Find out what type of show lead is proper and select one carefully.

SPORTING

The breeds in the Sporting Group were developed and used for hunting game. They are capable, attractive and devoted hunting companions. While the degree of discipline in training may vary, all of these dogs are properly handled in a gentle manner. The classic pose of a Sporting Dog should give the impression of a confident, well-mannered dog, willing and able to please its master.

All of the Sporting breeds are posed without lead. The handler kneels on one knee and holds the head and tail. A soft show lead (not a chain or choke) is preferable on Sporting breeds. One that is easily removed is best.

Read the standard for the breed you handle and use the information to understand proper handling. For example: The Golden Retriever has a "topline level from withers to croup." Therefore the Golden must be posed with a level topline. The English Setter has a "straight or very slightly sloping topline" and the English Springer "topline slopes very gently." These breeds must be posed in the manner described. The Irish Setter, the Pointer, the German Shorthair are described with a slight slope and are appropriately posed with more obvious height difference between withers and hipbone.

It is emphasized repeatedly in many of the Sporting Dog standards that ears shall be "at the same level as the eye," that "ears shall be carried well back, close to the head." There is also great emphasis placed on characteristics of face, head and expression. To pose these breeds correctly, then, it is necessary to remove the lead. The face, head, ears and neck must be featured. Never let a lead interfere with or change the proper lines of the dog.

The tail should be presented in the appropriate way. Make sure that your hands and fingers are used correctly. There are specific ways of holding the tails of various breeds. If the standard says that the tail "shall be in a horizontal position" or that it shall be carried on a line with a slightly sloping topline, that must be the way the tail is posed. Cocker handlers, please take note.

Sporting Dogs may be gaited on tight or loose lead. Make sure the speed is correct for your breed. Keys and squeakers are out of order here. They detract from the relaxed dignity of the dog. Use bait only if absolutely necessary when gaiting. Do not make it obvious. Never feed the dog bait in front of the judge. Don't pick up your Cocker in the ring except when putting it on the table. Don't carry a dog that should be an able hunter.

Debbie Stotyn is tickled with Setters.

Alison Stockland, handling her German Shorthaired Pointer to BOB, demonstrates proper pose. Note the tail is in a natural horizontal position—no hand needed.

63

Pat Leary LeMoigne advises, "The Afghan handler must try to match the grace and timing of the breed in motion. It takes great patience to coax the best from this breed. They cannot be forced. Use a light hand to guide them. Develop a sense of timing and rhythm in both moving and posing your dog. I used to hum to myself for improved timing."

HOUNDS

The breeds in the Hound Group were also developed to hunt. The scent Hounds and sight Hounds have very different jobs and so they differ greatly in appearance. From the dignified, aloof Afghan to the intelligent, audacious Dachshund, there is great variety and individuality among the Hounds.

A great variety of handling techniques also exists in the Hound breeds. In general the taller hounds are posed with the leads on—the Afghan, Irish Wolfhound, Borzoi. The smaller hounds are more properly presented without lead—the Beagle, Whippet, Dachshund. Choose a lead that is proper for the breed and comfortable for you to hold. It must be easily removed if you pose a breed without a lead. It must be easily gathered up into your hand if you pose on lead.

Study the standard for the breed you handle and then learn the correct way to pose your dog. It is necessary that you know the special characteristics of your breed so that you present them properly. It may be necessary for you to ask judges, breeders and handlers for help in perfecting your skill.

The Afghan is the only one of the large running hounds to be shown with the tail up. The flat of the fingers gently supports the tail in an upright position. Pose the Beagle and the Dachshund with plenty of room between handler and dog. Place your hand well under the head so you do not detract from face and head. Be careful that the Dachshund tail is a "continuation of the spine." The Beagle is posed with hind legs in a stance to show a level back and vertical hocks—never set out with a sloping topline. The Basset and Bloodhound have characteristic "wrinkles." Their standards also describe low set ears. Pose them with hand holding the head. The Norwegian Elkhound is appropriately posed on lead. Make sure you keep the lead the right length. The tail of the Whippet and Greyhound is characteristic. Position it properly.

When Juniors were still asked to exchange dogs in handling competition, a very successful young handler had to leave his Irish Setter to handle a Whippet. He later learned his mistake. But we often wonder how the Whippet felt with tail stretched straight out. Each breed must be gaited in its own special way. The Saluki must be a vision of grace and speed, the Basset a scenting dog, travels with his nose fairly low. After you have determined the best speed for your dog, learn to move with your dog without causing a break in gait. Bait may be helpful especially with the Basenji and the Elkhound, but be discreet.

BOB in Norwegian Elkhounds for Laura Mazzaro at Holyoke.

Bethny Brown, a third generation dog fancier, and her Ch. Beagle.

WORKING DOGS

Man has used dogs to help him with many tasks. The breeds developed to carry out these tasks are proud, courageous, alert and strong. The appearance of the Working Dog is always impressive. All breeds are on lead when posed.

Read the standard for the breed you handle. Find out what breed characteristics are important. Compare your dog to the standard and practice making the dog look its best. Get help from breed authorities on the fine points of handling. Choose the proper lead. There is a wide variety of gaiting styles among Working Dogs. The Old English Sheepdog has a distinctive ambling or pacing movement while the Great Dane moves with a long, easy, springy stride. Learn how and at what speed your dog should be moved.

Carry bait, keys or a toy. The finest handlers get their dogs' attention by suggesting bait with a hand in the pocket. In the same manner, a hidden squeaker is just as effective as one in sight. Continued use of these items is annoying to others.

Collie: The Collie handler must prepare his dog well to be able to present it properly in a natural position. The lead is used to guide the dog to stop in a proper pose. With the use of a fine choke chain collar and a nylon snap lead you can set the dog up just by applying pressure on the lead. If hand positioning of the rear feet is necessary it must be done in a subtle manner. The Collie handler must hold the lead so that the dog stands with neck slightly arched and upright. When posing the dog the handler stands at the side and holds the lead in the hand which is closest to the dog's rear. This leaves the hand nearest the dog's head free for keeping the dog alert.

The handler must present the dog in proper pose and at alert without distracting activity. Techniques used to alert the dog and set the ears erect are timed just before the judge's examination.

When showing the Collie the handler stands in front of the dog, and with as little activity as possible keeps the dog in pose and at alert.

Characteristic expression is very important and the able handler must use skill and perfect timing to have the dog look appealing at the necessary moment. The key to much of the success in handling this breed is to start show training early. Make it fun and establish a spirit of friendship with your dog.

Samoyed: This breed should be shown naturally. However, it is not a fault to hand pose your dog if it is necessary and you do it with smooth, effortless motions. Stand in front of your dog and keep it alert and eager. The special breed characteristic to be shown is the Sam smile. Gait the Samoyed on a loose lead

Lisa Kalmbrum smiling with her Samoyed.

First in Open JS at Twin Brooks for
George Russell and his Boxer.

and keep the dog in motion on turns by slowing the speed and using a wide turn.

Boxers and Dobermans are two of the Working breeds which may be posed by hand. Avoid unnecessary hand motions. The dog should give the impression of standing alone. Keep your lead hand close enough to the dog's head for control, but far enough away so that it does not detract from the view of the dog.

The German Shepherd Dog has a style and grace all its own. When gaiting this breed make sure *you* have correct posture and a proper stride.

Please, when you are standing in front of your dog appealing for his response, don't constantly use your knee to check his advance. This is unappealing and takes away from the overall impression you should be trying to achieve.

Ann Bowley says, "The Collie is a wonderful breed to work with—a pleasure to show and a joy to watch if the handler and dog make a graceful team."

Lisa Kalmbrum advises, "When you show a Samoyed wear dark clothing or bright solid colors to set off your dog. Never wear yellow and stay away from white—especially shoes."

Jodi Palmer and her Westie winning Open JS at Alberta.

TERRIERS

Fearless, incredibly active and clever are characteristics which mark the dogs bred to pursue vermin and small game. The Terriers more than any other group have a common personality trait. They possess boldness, determination and appear "full of fire."

A Terrier should be "handled" as little as possible. It should always appear that the dog is independent of the handler. All breeds are posed on lead. Choose a lead appropriate for your breed and especially for your individual dog. For example: A Resco show lead is excellent for a well mannered dog. A thin leather collar and nylon snap on lead is used for dogs which tend to "spin" or walk in circles. The swivel keeps the lead from getting twisted. A light weight martingale or choke collar is used only for very headstrong dogs.

Read the standard for the breed you handle. There are many

69

descriptions of Terriers which will help you understand the techniques necessary in handling. The Bull Terrier must show a "jaunty air," and the Australian Terrier is "of spirited action and self assured manner." The Cairn ". . . moves freely and easily on a loose lead" and shall "stand up on their toes and show with marked Terrier characteristics." Keenness of expression is mentioned in many of the standards. It is, therefore, necessary to show the keen eyes and alert, intelligent look of your Terrier.

The short-legged Terriers (Westie, Scottie, Border, etc.) are usually examined on the table. On the ground the small Terriers are properly presented in a free standing pose with the handler standing and working to keep the dog alert. The handler should kneel only if the dog will not stand with tail up for the judge's examination. Gait is proper on a loose lead. A "give and take" lead—one with some slack but more control—is also appropriate and recommended for JS classes.

The medium sized Terriers (Fox, Lakeland, Miniature Schnauzer) are usually examined on the table but at the judge's discretion. The proper handling techniques are the same as for the shorter breeds.

The large or heavy bodied Terriers (Airedale, Irish, Kerry, Bull) are examined on the ground and the handler stands when posing the dog. The same techniques of handling are proper with these breeds.

All Terrier breeds are properly shown on a loose lead or a "give and take" lead. A tight lead throws off the dog's movement and takes away from the independent Terrier look.

Remember, least handling is best. But there are many skills you must have to present a Terrier correctly. Your ability to keep your dog alert and responsive is important. Terriers should never be robot dogs that always appear in perfect stance. Their character and spirit must stand out.

Barbara Worcester Keenan (West Highland White Terriers) advises, "When deciding whether to set or drop a Terrier, determine which has the best results for your dog. The rear of the lighter-weight Terriers may be dropped by lifting from the base of the tail. This is not appropriate for the heavier breeds."

70

Edward Van Istendal says: "Sparring is only appropriate when done with another Terrier that is supposed to spar."

Deborah Duguid (Airedale) says, "When you handle the king of the Terriers make the dog look and feel like a king. When the judge comes to look at your dog, or when your dog has just finished gaiting, throw something on the ground to attract the dog. This will produce that alert expression and prick ears. At the end of gaiting it also helps bring the dog to an even stop. Win or lose, reward your dog in some way at the end of the class."

Merril Schmitt of Calgary winning JS First with her Cairn Terrier.

Terrier Techniques

Susan Hutchinson demonstrates the correct way to handle a Cairn Terrier. Many of the techniques are appropriate for all Terrier breeds.

1. Gently drop dog's front with hand under chest. If feet are out of place, set each foot by hand. Use left hand on left foot. Switch lead to left hand. Use right hand on right foot.

2. Set left rear foot, then right rear foot from behind. Note short lead for control in pose. Rear may also be set by dropping (holding base of tail). Check feet for proper placement.

3. Have dog alert and ready when judge examines from side. Hold tail up straight—never over back.

4. Call attention to Terrier expression when judge approaches from front. Stand at front of table and keep dog alert. Note short lead to prevent dog's moving.

5. Gait dog straight away from judge. Use loose lead. Carry bait or toy to keep dog's attention and head up.

6. Gait dog straight back to judge. Lead must be tighter for control to stop.

7. Walk dog into a free-standing pose on ground. Loose lead. Use bait to keep attention. Note Susan's per-fect posture and handling pose.

8. Correct Terrier pose, standing on his own.

9. Proper method for Terrier "spar" with another dog. Tight lead imperative for control. Keep distance if dogs are feisty.

The Do's And Don'ts of Handling a Maltese:

Daryl Martin demonstrates the special etiquette in handling a Maltese. Her Lhasa Apso models in several of the photos but the skills shown are appropriate to both breeds.

1. Correct handling of Toys on a table. Don't be on top of your dog. No unnecessary touching of dog. Keep proper distance. Hold leash properly. Keep brush out of view.

2. Improper handling on the table. Lead all over the dog. Overhandling of face and tail. Handler leaning directly on top of the dog obstructing judge's view.

3. Technique peculiar to Toy handling. Headstudy: call attention to a good head by holding the head gently so the judge can see it.

4. The improper way of showing the head. Handler is holding the head in an unnatural position. The dog's face is distorted. The fingers have lifted and disturbed the hair.

5. Proper gaiting. Lead not too short or too long. Keep your dog with you and alert to your wishes.

6. Improper gaiting. The dog is too far behind the handler. Lead is too long. Dog not properly gaited for the size and temperament.

7. Proper baiting technique. Hold bait slightly in front of dog but keep your body behind the dog to provide a contrasting background for the light dog. Hold the leash tightly on top of the dog to keep the neck high.

8. Improper baiting. This is a clumsy, unbalanced position. The handler detracts from the dog's stance.

1.

2.

3.

4.

5.

6.

7.

8.

TOY DOGS

The Toy breeds have existed for centuries and have remained popular as devoted companions. Once principally the delight of royalty and those of great wealth, the breeds in the Toy Group are varied in appearance. From the saucy little Chihuahua to the dramatic, beautiful Pekingese, to the slender, elegant Italian Greyhound, these dogs possess courage and intelligence. Because of their very small stature and the fact that they are properly posed on a table, Toys are difficult for use in JS.

The lead is not removed from the Toy when in pose. It is permissible for handlers to kneel on both knees when handling these breeds. However, keep the balls of your feet on the ground and do not kneel with your shins on the floor. Never move around your dog while in a kneeling position.

The proof that Juniors can win with Toys in JS is the success of Jennifer Hubbs. This California Junior also trained and handled her Papillon to CD.

NON-SPORTING DOGS

Most of the breeds in the Non-Sporting Group are unrelated. Their origins were linked to specific tasks, such as guarding, hunting or fighting. The appearance and temperament of the various breeds are as different as their origins. Contrast the Poodle's great beauty and air of distinction with the massive and courageous Bulldog. The breeds in the Non-Sporting Group are posed with leads on and, except for the larger dogs, the handler is usually in a kneeling position at the side of the dog.

Your choice of lead will probably be a Resco show lead or a light weight martingale. Study the standard for the breed you handle. Learn how to present your dog using handling techniques proper for the breed. Know how your individual dog looks best.

Bulldog: The task of the Bulldog handler is to create the overall impression of a massive, courageous yet peaceful dog.

Present the head with attention to details peculiar to the breed. The lead is placed on the neck so that the two loose pendulous folds between jaw and chest are prominent. The hand holding the lead should be out of the immediate area of the dog's head. The free hand may be used to guide the head to a face forward position or to check the lay of the flews or the chops.

The front feet of the Bulldog are positioned so that the legs are straight from the elbow to the foot, when viewed from the front. From the side, the legs fall in a straight line between withers and feet. Elbows are well out away from the body. The rear feet are positioned so that the rear legs form an almost straight line from hip bones to feet when viewed from the side. The hock is only slightly bent. From the rear, the feet are wide apart to allow sufficient width between the turned out stifles. Bulldog handlers must note that it is characteristic to have hocks turned slightly toward each other and rear feet turned outward.

Dalmatian: Strong, muscular, active and capable of great endurance with a fair amount of speed describes the Dalmatian. Pose this breed by hand. Place the forelegs straight and under the dog for appropriate angulation. The hindquarters are placed to show a powerful, slightly arched back and to emphasize the balance and strength of the rear. Do not exaggerate the stance of the Dalmatian. The nose must be on slightly lower plane than the eye so that the neck appears nicely arched. Hold the tail in a slight upward curve. Place the hand under the tail at a point beyond the middle. Gait this breed in a steady rhythm.

Cody Sickle and his Bulldog, Cherokee Morgan.

Christine McFadden prepares her Standard Poodle for JS at Harrisburg.

6/Let's Play
Twenty Questions

THE questions in this chapter are some of those most often asked by juniors. These questions have been taken from the letters we have received over the past 17 years.

1. How can I find a pen pal who is interested in dogs?

The major magazines which have JS columns compile a list of pen pals regularly. Send your name, address, age and breed interest to the columnist.

Did you know that Lydia Coleman Hutchinson and Marsha Hall Brown were pen pals before they met in the JS ring?

2. Why are dogs "handled?"

Dogs are "presented," "handled" or "shown" so that the judge can examine and observe each entry thoroughly and without delay. The handler is providing a service and showing courtesy by making the judge's examination as easy as possible.

3. Just what is Junior Showmanship?

Junior Showmanship Competition is the class at a dog show at which the handling merits of junior contestants are judged.

4. Who can judge JS?

Any person who is eligible to judge one or more breeds. Any former Junior Showmanship competitor approved by the AKC to judge JS.

5. Why don't all shows have JS?

It is the decision of the show-giving clubs to include JS classes. Unfortunately some clubs do not realize the importance of JS.

6. What other countries have JS?

Australia, Canada, and Great Britain.

7. How can we start a junior kennel club?

How to form the club:

Go to your nearest kennel club (breed or all-breed) and ask them to approve a junior division. (All junior clubs should be affiliated with an adult organization.)

The kennel club should appoint an adult chairman and/or committee to help and advise the junior group.

All interested juniors should be invited to join. Hold a "planning" meeting. The junior club should elect officers with the assistance of adult advisors. Junior officers and adult advisors should study the by-laws of the parent club and work out suitable by-laws for their junior division.

Set a membership fee. Make it reasonable in amount.

Juniors should plan and carry out their own club activities. The adult chairman and/or committee should serve in an advisory capacity.

8. Our breed club would like to encourage juniors. What is the best way we can do this?

1. Provide Junior Showmanship information to the young people in the club and if possible organize a class of instruction for them.

2. Offer an annual award for the best Junior Showman in the club.

3. Include junior news in club newsletters, bulletins or magazines.

4. Offer JS Competition at your club match and speciality show. Do not charge an entry fee.

9. Can a female in season be handled in Junior Showmanship?

Yes. However, we strongly recommend that tablets and sprays be used for the dog to minimize the problem. Only an experienced and completely responsible junior should be expected to compete under these conditions. If there is any evidence that the dog's presence in the ring is disruptive or presents a danger to the safety of other dogs or juniors, the junior handling the bitch in season should leave the ring. Notify the ring steward that the bitch is in season. Many times the best position in the ring is last in line or among other bitches.

80

10. Our Junior Kennel Club is compiling a library for members' use. Can you suggest some helpful books for juniors?

Dog Care and Training for Boys and Girls, by Blanche Saunders

Dog Training for Kids, by Carol Benjamin

The Complete Dog Book, The American Kennel Club

International Encyclopedia of Dogs, Howell Book House

The AKC Rules Applying to Registrations and Dog Shows and *The AKC Regulations for Junior Showmanship* are a must.

Junior Showmanship columns appear in *Kennel Review Magazine, The American Kennel Gazette,* and *Dog World.* These columns are helpful and informative. Donald Sturz, a successful junior competitor, writes for Kennel Review.

Your local library can suggest books of dog fiction.

11. I have been entering JS at point shows. Am I still eligible for Junior Showmanship at match shows?

Yes. However, after you have placed consistently at point shows it would be a courtesy for you to limit your match handling to the breed ring.

12. I am in charge of trophies for an all-breed club. Please suggest prizes for Junior Showmanship.

We humbly suggest that this Handbook would make a very appropriate prize. Pen and pencil sets, scrapbooks and photo albums are popular with juniors. Dog items such as leads, tie clasps and pins are also appreciated but a gift certificate at a "show shop" is even better. The most thoughtful thing a club can do is to reward every junior who does not win or place with a token of some kind. Candy, ball point pens, pads and even gift-wrapped Milkbones have been given at shows.

13. Is there any age limit for juniors handling in regular breed classes?

No. However, it is important that the junior be experienced enough to have full control over his or her dog. Also it is only common courtesy to the judge that the junior be competent enough to handle the dog and to follow directions.

14. I am going to several shows in Canada. Will I be able to compete in Junior Showmanship?

Yes. Junior Showmanship is very similar to competition here.

15. I show a toy breed and I am used to posing my dog on a table for examination. Many of the JS judges neglect to use a table. What can I do?

Before any of the JS classes have begun ask the ring steward if a table can be provided for small breeds. When the steward asks the judge where the table should be placed, it will be a "reminder" to use it.

16. I have heard that there is a scholarship fund for deserving junior dog fanciers. Is that true?

Yes. First named after George F. Foley and in honor of his 80th birthday, the fund began in 1962. Renamed the Exhibitor's Educational Trust, it is now the Dog Writers Education Trust. Applicants are judged on scholastic ability, participation in the dog fancy, character, and financial need. The fund operates entirely on contributions from organizations and individuals in the sport of dogs. For applications or donations write: The Dog Writers Educational Trust, Mrs. Robert Futh, Secretary, Kinney Hill Road, Washington Depot, Connecticut 06794.

17. My dog is purebred and can be entered at shows but he is not show quality. It is the only dog I have for Junior Showmanship. What can I do?

Under the present Junior Showmanship rules a dog can be entered for "JS Only" as long as it is eligible for shows. However, it would be to your advantage to have another dog to handle. Many breeders and exhibitors are very interested in helping juniors and are sometimes willing to give deserving juniors co-ownership in a dog. Talk to other members of your breed club or write to its secretary or junior chairman. Many times, juniors earn the privilege of co-ownership by helping in the kennels, exercising dogs and assisting the owner at shows.

A Junior Showmanship dog, our Bo'Sun, was handled to title by both of us. He was also handled in Junior Showmanship over the years by Charles Capace, Betty Lou Ham, Sally Sly, Laurel Howe and Elizabeth and Bethny Brown.

18. Why don't juniors stop competing in Junior Showmanship after they have compiled their qualifying wins for Westminster?

Junior Showmanship is a success because it is an open competition based on initiative and personal achievement. A junior may compete as little or as often as he wishes. He may exhibit any breed he owns. Most important, he has the right to accumulate as many wins as he or she is able. If a junior cannot qualify for Westminster, he or she has not earned the honor of being there. Dogs in competition are not limited only to a share of wins and then retired to allow other dogs to score. Annual awards are based on consistent achievement throughout the year. Juniors must compete often and win often to receive such awards.

19. How can I get a job working in a show kennel for the summer?

Write to kennels in your area stating your age, experience and interest in dogs. An advertisement in a large all-breed or breed club newsletter might be helpful. Professional handlers often need extra help in the summer months. Write to handlers near you, or discuss your work interest with handlers at shows when they are not busy. You might also consider work in an animal hopsital or grooming shop. Read your local newspaper for help wanted listings.

20. Are certain breeds easier to win with in Junior Showmanship than other breeds?

A highly skilled junior will win in Junior Showmanship regardless of the breed of dog being handled. It is true, however, that there are certain breeds (Setters, Pointers, Afghans, Doberman Pinschers, Boxers, to name a few) that are eye-catching. These breeds provide a good opportunity for the junior to demonstrate handling skill. The breeds most difficult for use in Junior Showmanship are the very large and the very small. It is a difficult job to cope with a Newfoundland and look relaxed as well as competent. It is even more difficult to "shine" with a Toy breed. Rarely are juniors judged on table handling etiquette which is the major skill in showing a Toy.

It is interesting to note that juniors have won with just about every breed. Some juniors have turned a seemingly difficult breed into their chief asset by becoming so skillful that the dog looks remarkable. The best example of this is the great success of Cody Sickle and his Bulldogs. He made those Bulldogs outclass the merriest Setter and the most dignified Dobe.

Peter and Heidi Martin winning their Junior Showmanship classes. The Martins: Bryan, Peter and Heidi have qualified for Westminster for twelve consecutive years 1967–78. Now both Bryan and Peter are Junior Showmanship Judges.

It's a real family affair—Melissa Butt, Dionne Butt and Jennifer Butt. The three Butt sisters have a total of 160 Junior wins.

7/Particularly for Parents

TO be the parent of a Junior Showmanship competitor is physically, emotionally and financially taxing. You have, no doubt, often wondered whether you will survive the next competition.

While your junior is at a school pep rally, you are making out the entries and checks for the next show. A special scout meeting is called for the night the dogs are to be bathed and the car packed. And your junior, so exhausted from the merry whirl of activity during the week, sleeps for the three hours it takes you to drive to the show. Then, while your junior becomes completely involved in handling (with varying degrees of skill) in Junior Showmanship you can only stand nervously at ringside and try not to talk to yourself or weep in public.

To be the parent of a Junior Showmanship competitor is also a treasured experience and a great pride. To help your own child practice, and master the skill of handling a dog you are both fond of, is the beginning of a mutual interest. The travel, the grooming, exercising, and waiting are never time measured in hours or minutes but in "time together." The first time your junior does a good job of handling, or gets a placing, or finally wins the pink ribbon, there is much to share. And when your junior qualifies for Westminster, or wins an annual award, or finishes a champion, you will find that your time and work and moments of disappointment are overshadowed completely by the pride and joy in your junior's accomplishment.

Words to the Wise

Before great plans are made for junior competition, a parent must determine whether the junior wants to handle and whether the junior is ready for competition.

Father and son combination at the shows: William P. Gilbert ("Mr. Great Dane") and William J. Gilbert.

A junior should enter Junior Showmanship only if:

He or she can control the dog at all times.
He or she has some knowledge of ring procedure and can follow the directions of the judge.
The junior is emotionally mature enough to understand and accept winning or losing.
The junior likes dogs and is thoughtful of his dog's well-being.
The junior wishes to participate.

Wise parents will help the junior at practice sessions at home and encourage handling at match shows first. When the junior enters competition the parent must assume the role of guide and advisor only. If there is a question for the judge or ring steward before or after the competition, the junior should seek the answer.

Thoughtful parents will praise the junior immediately following competition for all the good points demonstrated and refrain from any criticism until the next practice session at home. To teach the junior the ideals of sportsmanship the parent must practice good sportsmanship. The wise parent should try to limit the discussion of competition to the positive aspects involved. Pointing out other juniors who are competent or who perform a particular skill well, and discussing the judges who are helpful and thorough, make constructive conversation.

When a particular competition is difficult and not successful for the junior, a helpful parent can guide the junior's thoughts to the next show and the next chance in the ring.

Parents should encourage their juniors to congratulate the winner of Junior Showmanship classes. Juniors should also receive some instruction from parents concerning appropriate manners when they win.

The practical parent will help the junior learn about care, health and training of dogs. Daily responsibilities for juniors are recommended. Simple chores should be the task of beginning juniors, and older or more experienced juniors should be capable of more difficult duties.

The understanding parent will know that it is necessary for a junior to enjoy activities in other fields. The parent should encourage participation in sports and hobbies, membership in youth groups, and time spent at social activities at school or in the community.

Sense and Sensibility

Of course the parent provides the junior with the dog, financial support, transportation and a cheering section of at least one. But the responsibility of a parent is not that simple.

There are rules governing Junior Showmanship. Every junior must know these rules and follow them. The parent must see to it that his or her junior is honoring all rules.

The parent is responsible for the appearance and demeanor of the junior. Planning and preparation at home will help the junior realize the importance of appropriate attire and the necessity of good manners.

The safety of all juniors in competition is the responsibility of the parents of those juniors. The parent must be certain that the junior he or she sends into Junior Showmanship has the knowledge and physical ability to control the dog at all times, especially in crowded conditions. The dog must be considered. A parent must choose a dog of stable temperament and be sure it is suitable for a young person to handle. The parent should

87

Dog shows make for togetherness. Rebecca and Jonathan Mason prepare for a show with their friend Christine McFadden. *Ray Mason*

also instruct the junior in the thoughtful treatment of the dog both in and out of the show ring.

Help Wanted

Parents can help juniors and Junior Showmanship most by:

Helping the all-breed clubs provide for Junior Showmanship at shows.

Offering trophies or prizes for Junior Showmanship classes; submitting a list of knowledgeable and available judges for Junior Showmanship classes.

Encouraging a breed club to offer annual junior awards for juniors handling that breed in Junior Showmanship and regular classes.

Offering obedience and field awards.

Offering time or financial support to insure the continued success of the club's annual junior award.

Extending a helping hand to parents and juniors just beginning.

Being good sports themselves.

Keeping a sense of humor.

8/You Can Be A Six-Star Junior

FOR Junior Kennel Clubs as well as for juniors everywhere this is a program of learning. This basic outline can be simplified, shortened, modified or added to so as to meet the needs of the group's interests and age range. It is intended to help juniors become more aware of a great variety of dog-related activities. It is also aimed at preparing juniors to be of service in a variety of ways to "Man's Best Friend."

MEET . . . GO . . . SAVE . . . HELP . . . DIG . . . DO . . . are the six units of activity. To complete a unit, choose five of the suggested activities and carry them out. When a junior completes all six units, he or she shall be a Six-Star Junior.

MEET!

This activity unit is to help make club meetings different and interesting and to encourage all members to participate.

Complete five of the following (numbers 1 and 5 are required):

1. Be in charge of planning for at least one meeting.
2. Present part of the program at a meeting.
3. Teach a skill.
4. Know how to introduce a speaker, welcome a guest or new member.
5. Give a book report or read a short article from a magazine or newspaper on a dog-related topic.
6. Be in charge of ordering a film to show at a meeting.
7. Make up a simple game or quiz for members to play.
8. Demonstrate a simple handling or training technique.
9. Plan a panel discussion.
10. Plan and help prepare a debate.

GO!

This activity unit includes suggested field trips. Choose five from the following (number 3 is required):

1. Visit a dog officer or dog warden.
2. Visit a Humane Society, dog shelter or pound.
3. Visit a veterinary hospital.
4. Visit an established kennel.
5. Visit or take part in a dog training class.
6. Visit the working place of a professional in the field of dogs. Example: handler, groomer, photographer, artist, etc.
7. Attend a show, trial or other organized dog event.
8. Visit a pet shop.
9. Take snapshots of one of your trips and make a scrapbook.
10. Go to a museum or art gallery and discover dogs as presented by artists.

SAVE!

This activity unit is most important for all juniors. Dog health, safety and first aid knowledge is necessary for all dog fanciers. The help of a veterinarian is suggested for some of these activities. Choose five of the following (numbers 1, 3 and 6 are required):

1. Know how to groom and trim your dog properly. Know why it is essential to care for nails, teeth, ears and coat.
2. Learn the proper diet for your dog and know how much exercise your dog needs daily.
3. Find out what diseases your dog is susceptible to and learn how to prevent them. Know what internal and external parasites might affect your dog's health. Learn how to control these problems.
4. Show that you can take a dog's temperature and administer medicine in liquid or tablet form.
5. Discuss the proper way to bathe a dog. Bathe your own dog. Know how to use powder and liquid preparations for removal of fleas, ticks or lice.
6. Be able to give first aid for the following: wounds, internal injuries, electric shock, fractures, hemorrhage, burns, shock, drowning, suffocation and animal bites.
7. Know the first aid and proper medical treatment for a person who has been bitten by a dog.

8. Make an emergency muzzle and show how to use it. Know the use of a dog lasso and restraining stick.
9. Know how to approach an injured dog and what safety precautions are necessary for you and the dog.
10. Know the care of a brood bitch and learn how to care for a newborn litter.
11. Learn the laws in your community and state concerning dog ownership, dog control and unclaimed dogs. Know how to contact the nearest animal shelter.
12. Find out the humane and professional method for destroying animals.

HELP

This activity unit is to introduce juniors to the many fields of dog services and to help juniors be of service. Choose five of the following (number 5 is required):

1. Find out how stray and/or injured animals are cared for in your area. If possible, visit the nearest shelter. Learn the local and state laws which pertain to unclaimed dogs.
2. Find out how and why dogs are licensed in your area. What are the fees and how are they collected and used?
3. Learn how guide dogs are selected and trained for the blind.
4. Learn how dogs are used in one of the following categories: police work, military service, search, guarding (schools and buildings.)
5. Participate in one of the following suggested activities, or with your group select a project or activity which would be of service to your area. Give at least 20 hours of your time to this project.
   a. Organize, help to organize or work at a town rabies clinic.
   b. Help your town or city with dog licensing by helping to take a dog census, or do simple office work.
   c. With your parent club or members of the parent club plan and carry out a dog demonstration at a school, hospital or children's home.
   d. Volunteer to help your local Humane Society.
   e. With your parent club or members of the parent club plan and carry out a public demonstration for Dog Week or Be Kind to Animals Week.
   f. Find out what services the following groups provide: Orthopedic Foundation for Animals, Humane Society of the United States, American Society for the Prevention of Cruelty to Animals, The Seeing Eye.

DIG

This activity unit is to help juniors understand and appreciate the dog today by digging into the past.

Choose five of the following (numbers 1 and 8 are required):

1. Study the basic structure of the dog. Learn the parts of the dog by name. Study the skeletal formation of the dog and know the names of the major bones.
2. Read about the earliest history of the dog and find out what animal group it belongs to.
3. Find out how purebred dogs originated. Learn the origin of your favorite breed and how it has developed to the present day.
4. Learn how man has used dogs for specific purposes in the past. Know at least four main uses of the dog today.
5. Read about famous dogs in history.
6. Read at least one book about a dog.
7. Know three authors noted for their dog stories. Read about one of these authors.
8. Learn the AKC standard for your favorite breed. Explain it at a club meeting.
9. Become familiar with three famous works of art featuring the dog. Know the artists' names and when the paintings or sculptures were done.

DO

This unit is to help juniors learn more about and participate in organized dog activities. Choose five of the following (number one is required):

1. Participate in one of the major fields of the dog activity (show, obedience or field.) Learn to handle and become familiar with the rules of the competition.
2. Learn how to make out an entry form and how to mark a catalog.
3. With members of your club or with the parent club plan and carry out a match show, fun field trial, or handling competition.
4. Select a field of activity (other than the one you specialize in) and learn more about it. Attend a show or trial.
5. Find out about other regular dog activities such as herding, drill teams, hound packs, racing, dog sled racing, and tracking and search. Find out about the handling and training of some of these.
6. Know how a dog earns title in your selected field or activity.
7. Compare shows or trials in the United States with those held in another country.
8. Find out the regulations pertaining to the shipping of dogs by air.

Nancy Brick, Animal Health Technician introduces an-esthesia. *Photo courtesy of Foothill College*

9/Looking Ahead . . . Careers for You

HAVE you thought of how dogs will fill your future? Have you ever considered filling your future with dogs? Your interest and experience as a junior fancier can be a valuable first step toward a career of life-long avocation. The following opportunities in dog-related fields include professional and semi-professional careers, full time and part-time occupations, and leisure time involvement.

Veterinary Medicine

There are many and varying career opportunities for a Doctor of Veterinary Medicine. Aside from private practice, either individually or in groups, the DVM may choose research, teaching, public health work, meat inspection, disease control, or conservation and ecology. Veterinarians are employed by universities, hospitals and laboratories. They work for the federal, state and local governments, with the Peace Corps and the military. Drug companies and dog food companies need qualified doctors on their staffs. The Atomic Energy Commission and the National Aeronautics and Space Administration also employ veterinarians.

There are only 22 veterinary schools in the United States. All the schools have a limited number of admissions each year. At the University of California at Davis only 94 students are accepted annually in the beginning class. Admission may be further limited by a state resident requirement.

You can find the list of Veterinary Schools at your public library or from your high school or college counselor. For admission requirements write to the school and request a college catalogue or brochure of the veterinary school.

The basic requirements are:

1. A college preparatory high school course with emphasis on science and math.
2. Undergraduate work in an accredited college or university including the required courses outlined by the veterinary school.
3. Outstanding academic achievement.
4. Substantial experience with animals. Working with a veterinarian is ideal.

It takes between six and eight years to become a DVM. Four years of veterinary school is preceded by two, three and sometimes four years of college training. This career demands high scholastic ability, hard work, determination and dedication to science and animals. It is interesting and exciting work with personal and financial rewards.

Animal Health

The fastest growing career opportunities in dog related fields are in Animal Health. Trained technicians are assistants to veterinarians and scientists. They perform laboratory tests, prepare animals and instruments for surgery and assist in surgery and other medical procedures. Technicians also dress and care for wounds, do radiography, record keeping and general animal care. They work in all fields where veterinarians are employed. Medical centers, research institutions, government health agencies, animal hospitals and clinics are the most common.

Training for this work is now offered in 34 states and two Canadian provinces. Most programs are two year courses resulting in an associate degree. Several colleges offer a four year course of study which leads to a bachelor of science degree.

Basic requirements are:

1. College preparatory high school course with emphasis in math and science.
2. Grade average and SAT scores sufficient for college entrance.
3. Experience in animal care and maintenance. Raising animals, work in kennels or a veterinary hospital are highly recommended.

Animal Health Technicians are in great demand. There are many and varied career opportunities. Salaries are commensurate.

The most complete listing of colleges and universities which offer Animal Health courses is in *Pure-Bred Dogs—American Kennel Gazette*, June 1976.

Dog Photographer

The dog photographer must be highly skilled in his or her profession, must enjoy dogs and people, must possess endless patience, and must be willing to travel. Dog photographers must also have a basic knowledge of breed characteristics and proper show poses.

There are official photographers at all dog shows. These professionals are listed in the show catalog by the show giving club. They perform two basic services. They record on film the winners of the show from Best of Breed to Best in Show.

They also are available at the dog owner's request to record other wins or activities of the day.

This area of dog photography is difficult work. Long hours must be spent traveling and working away from home on weekends. Clear photos must be produced regardless of weather, lighting or show sites. Developing and mailing keep the photographer working long hours between shows. Often dog owners and magazines request rush orders for photos of show wins in order to meet publication deadlines.

Dog photographers work in a variety of other places. Many schedule private appointments for special pictures and portraits

Bill Gilbert, Junior Showman, Assistant Handler, Licensed Handler, Official Dog Show Photographer. Bill began his photographic career with training he received in the United States Navy.

during the week. A photographer may be hired by a large kennel to record on film the various dogs in residence. Several noted dog photographers specialize in taking unusual candids of children and dogs. Photographers are in demand to cover such dog related events as obedience, field and retriever trials, herding events and tracking and search tests.

Many dog photographers work in advertising. From dog food to grooming supplies to medical preparations, photographs of dogs are used to sell most products.

A career in photography can be interesting and financially rewarding. Professional training, practical experience and knowledge of dogs are all necessary prerequisites. After high school graduation the future photographer should seek enrollment in a technical school, college or night school which offers a complete program in photography. Experience in simple photography can be gained by taking pictures for school clubs, newspapers, socials and sports events. Taking photos at dog training classes, handling classes and match shows can be a learning experience. The study and observations of animals and dogs is important. The future dog photographer should attend shows and other dog events and visit kennels.

Dog Training

The variety of careers and employment opportunities for the dog trainer is almost endless. Man uses the dog in so many ways and in so many places that capable dog trainers are always in great demand.

Obedience training for dogs has become very popular not only as a basic service to the pet owner but to the obedience trial enthusiast. Training classes and obedience schools are sponsored by towns and organizations all over the country. Instructors at these schools teach owners how to train their dogs. There are also professional trainers who own or work for private dog training schools. These dog trainers work primarily with dogs sent for training.

Dogs are used for hunting, racing and herding and must be trained accordingly. Training kennels are maintained where dogs may be sent for field trial training, retriever trial training and for breaking gun dogs and hunting hounds. Racing dogs also require special training. Herding dogs are a great aid to livestock owners, and large ranches many times employ a trainer and handler for the dogs.

There are dog trainers in the entertainment field. Any time dogs appear in plays, movies, and on television, it represents long hours of work on the part of a skilled trainer.

Valerie Fisher, of Seattle, Washington, the youngest handler in history to train and handle a dog to Field Trial championship, gives a command to her famous AFTC Misty's Sungold Lad, CDX. This amazing young trainer has taken the most coveted national awards for field work. She is also an accomplished obedience trainer.

The greatest service the dog provides for man is as a guide for the blind. The most highly skilled trainers are necessary for work in programs like The Seeing Eye. They must work with the dogs, the future owners and the staff specialists.

Guard and sentry dogs are trained for use in the military, for police work and for private use. Most of the professional dog trainers in this category have received their career training and experience while serving in the armed forces. Those trainers who leave the military often are employed by state or local police.

Dogs must be trained for patrol duty, search and criminal apprehension. In recent years dogs have been trained and used as reliable narcotics "agents." They have been used at customs stations, post offices and shipping ports.

Tracking dogs are also trained and used by police. Bloodhounds have led police to many suspects and have found many injured or lost people. Trainers are needed to supply the growing demand for guard dogs in schools and industries.

There are so many different and specialized careers in dog training that it is impossible to include information on instruction and preparation. However, it is advisable to learn basic training procedures by gaining experience in obedience work. It would also be helpful to seek summer employment or part-time employment at a kennel or school where dogs are trained for some type of work. Many young people, particularly 4-H Club members, volunteer to provide foster homes for future guide dogs.

Dog Artist

"Stop, Look, and Listen" is the advice to the junior who aspires to be a dog artist. Before you take pen and ink or brush and canvas in hand, stop and take the time to observe all forms of animal life. Watch both wild and tamed animals in their natural settings while in motion. Observe the difference between the old and the young, the male and the female. Look at dogs of all breeds. Educate your eye by training, trimming and caring for dogs. Study breed characteristics and coat textures. Then listen to some practical advice.

Patricia Detmold, well-known for her water colors of animals and wild life, specializes in dog portraits. Pat won her first Children's Handling class at her first competition in Montreal, Quebec, Canada in 1946. She has successfully bred, trained and handled Sporting dogs for show, field and obedience.

A career as an artist, especially when it is limited to animals and wildlife, might be a financial risk in the beginning. The future dog artist should take basic art courses in high school and plan further study at a college, technical school or art school which offers a well-rounded program. Commercial art and art education graduates will find interesting employment opportunities and be able to work in the field of dog art in spare time.

To be successful, the dog artist must have some background in biology, anatomy, animal and dog history, breed characteristics, and technical art skills. Remember: the artist must be able to produce quality work and satisfying likenesses. The artist also must be able to portray hunting dogs afield and working dogs on the job.

Professional Dog Handler

A professional dog handler grooms, conditions, trains and shows dogs for other people and is paid for his or her services. The successful handler is a specialist in the field of dogs, a good businessman and a tireless traveler. Since almost all dog shows are scheduled on weekends, the handler spends almost the entire week on the job. It is a difficult and demanding career. But the variety provided by the dogs, clients, travel and contemporaries makes it most interesting.

Preparation—Since there is no school or training program, it is the task of the individual to prepare for this work. It is essential to be experienced in the sport of dogs and to attain a high degree of skill as a trainer, handler, conditioner and groomer. This knowledge can be acquired through employment with an established breeding kennel or a professional handler's kennel. A fundamental knowledge of running a business, keeping records and handling correspondence is necessary. The future handler must also know about canine health, maintenance and first aid. Driving experience, including city and freeway situations and a valid driver's license, are musts. AKC rules and regulations must be studied.

The Professional Handlers Association is an organization of experienced handlers interested in the betterment of dog activities throughout the country. The PHA has a Code of Ethics and publishes information for members on business, management and handling.

PHA membership applicants must be at least 21 years old and in good standing with the AKC. They must have a minimum of three years' experience as a handler formerly licensed by the AKC which discontinued licensing handlers on January 1, 1978, submit photos and drawings of kennel facilities, and complete a PHA application form. Those who have not been licensed handlers but have experience for at least five years in a show dog related field (breeder, handler's assistant, veterinary assistant) may submit a Letter of Intent to the PHA Board of Governors. This letter will be filed for a period of at least one year before application may be made.

Assistant Handler

Future handlers may train for their profession by working as an assistant handler under the supervision of an experienced and established handler.

4-M Enterprises, Inc.

1280 PACIFIC STREET
UNION CITY, CALIFORNIA 94587
(510) 489-8722 - Office
(510) 489-8331 - Fax

Date _8/13_, 19_94_

Name _Laurie Jordan_

Address _____

City _____

STATE   ZIP CODE

QUANTITY	TITLE OR BREED	AUTHOR	PRICE
1	Book		15 00

TOTAL FOR ORDER _____

CALIFORNIA RESIDENTS ADD 8.25% SALES TAX _____

MAILING CHARGES _____

TOTAL _15 00_

AMOUNT RECEIVED _15_

C.O.D. OR BALANCE _____

ORDER COMPLETE _____

NP   NOT YET RELEASED FROM THE PUBLISHER
OP   OUT OF PRINT. DISCONTINUED
OS   TEMPORARILY OUT OF STOCK, WILL SHIP WHEN READY
SOO   SPECIAL ORDER ONLY - WILL SHIP WHEN IN STOCK

THANK YOU FOR ALLOWING US TO SERVE YOU

Charlotte Stacy says it best, "My advice to anyone wanting to make showing dogs a profession would be to work for an established handler to learn how to operate a business. There is more to being a successful professional handler than walking in the ring and showing a dog. The knowledge of conditioning animals is a most important part of being successful."

Charlotte Martin Stacy is an all-breed handler who specializes in Cocker Spaniels. She and her husband Terry, both former Juniors, are now parents of Juniors. The Stacys' Kennel in Virginia is the home of many BIS Cockers.

George Alston, 1954 Westminster winner, teaches handling classes for Juniors and adults. He and his wife Mary Ann are successful handlers. Their Fieldstone Kennels is in Maryland.

Holliston Junior College in Lenox, Mass. offers courses in kennel management and dog care as well as show and obedience handling. Photo courtesy of *Pure-Bred Dogs-AKC Gazette*

Dog Care

There are many career and business opportunities in the field of dog care. Boarding and grooming establishments employ many people. Humane Societies and dog pounds must be staffed by skilled workers. Veterinarians and animal hospitals need non-professional help. The newest business in this area of work is the dog walker.

The owner and operator of a boarding kennel must have the proper facilities for keeping dogs and must know the state and town ordinances for kenneling dogs. He or she must be responsible, experienced in the care of dogs, and capable of keeping dogs healthy and the facilities clean and in good repair.

Kennel workers must like dogs and demonstrate responsibility in caring for them. Duties will include feeding, providing water and cleaning kennel areas.

A professional dog groomer must be skilled not only in proper trimming and bathing methods but must have knowledge of breed standards and basic canine anatomy. To be successful a groomer must also know how to cope with unruly animals and those not accustomed to electric clippers, nail clippers and tools used to clean teeth and ears. A future groomer must learn how to care for the variety of tools and equipment used and how to keep them clean.

Several states now have excellent schools of dog grooming. The New York School of Dog Grooming was the first and is licensed by the State Department of Education. It offers three courses: instruction for pet owners, the basic course for professional groomers and the advanced course. The duration of the professional course is one month. The curriculum also includes instruction for future grooming shop owners and managers.

Many of the job opportunities in dog care provide on-the-job training. Young people can gain valuable experience by working at kennels, animal hospitals or grooming shops during summer vacations or on a part-time basis.

It is important that applicants for these jobs have high school diplomas or the equivalent and have good character references. For those who plan to be self employed and especially for those who will be employing others, a basic course in business is recommended.

Dog Show Judge

There are approximately 2,700 men and women who are approved by the AKC to judge at dog shows. These authorities perform the task of evaluating the conformation and gait of the dog. The judge must examine each dog and determine how it "measures up" to the written standard for its breed. Then the judge must decide which dog comes closest to the standard description. Some judges are eligible only for obedience classes.

Some judges are approved by the AKC to judge only one or two different breeds. Others may judge all the breeds in one of the six groups. There are also judges, called all-rounders, who judge all recognized breeds.

The great majority of judges donate their time and services or request a fee which will simply cover expenses to and from

Former Junior and one of America's youngest BIS judges, Lydia Coleman Hutchinson poses with her choice at Eastern Dog Club, Boston, Mass.

the show. In most cases, only those judges who are qualified to judge many breeds and are long experienced receive fees of a professional nature.

The role of a judge requires long experience, study and knowledge of all phases of the dog fancy. The judging of dogs is fascinating and rewarding. However, long hours in the ring under all kinds of weather conditions make this job physically and mentally tiring.

Application for judging eligibility may be requested from the AKC. Any person over the age of twenty-one who is in good standing with the AKC and has had experience in purebred dogs may apply. The applicant must be prepared to list personal statistics, give a reason for wishing to judge and submit records of breeding and showing. He or she must also write about the breed or breeds applied for and answer questions about the AKC rules and regulations.

If the name of the applicant is authorized for publication it will appear in the next issue of *Pure-bred Dogs—The American Kennel Gazette.* Two months after the original publication the AKC Board of Directors will act upon the application and if it is approved, the name of the applicant will be listed as "provisional judge." After the completion of three judging assignments the applicant must wait for the board to make a final review. If it is a favorable action the applicant becomes a judge.

Junior Showmanship Judge

In 1974 the AKC began approving qualified former Junior Showmanship competitors as judges for the JS classes. This new addition to Junior competition has provided many knowledgeable and competent judges for the JS classes.

Application to judge JS may be requested from the AKC. The applicant must be 17 years of age or over and be experienced in JS competition. Information requested by the AKC includes:

1. When did you first compete in JS?
2. List JS awards won by you during last two years as a competitor.
3. Have you judged JS at matches?
4. List activities in the sport of dogs since JS competition.
5. Give two personal references.
6. Describe the judging procedure for a class of 15.

If the name of the applicant is authorized for publication it will appear in *Pure-Bred Dogs—The American Kennel Gazette*. Two months later the AKC Board of Directors will act upon the application and if approved, the name of the applicant will be listed as Provisional Junior Showmanship Judge. After the completion of three judging assignments the applicant must wait for the board to make a final decision. If the decision is favorable the new judges name will be published under New Junior Showmanship Judges, Provisional completed.

Pamela Brink, approved Junior Showmanship Judge, presenting Best Junior Handler of California award to Diane Haywood at Sun Maid KC.

Pure-Bred Dog Breeder

The fundamental role in the sport of dogs is that of the breeder. It is the most difficult role and many times the most discouraging. It can also be the most rewarding. The future of purebred dogs is in the hands of those who spend their leisure time as breeders.

There are no formal qualifications, but the following will serve as a guide to those interested in this field.

A conscientious breeder must have one basic goal—to improve the quality of his chosen breed. Those who would breed dogs for the fun of it, or as an experiment, are selfish. Those who think only in terms of producing litters to sell are cruel (humane societies report regularly on the critical problems of canine overpopulation.) Those who continue haphazard trial and error methods are a detriment to the breed.

The breeding of dogs is not a self supporting hobby. The financial responsibility must be met and understood. The price of a quality brood bitch is high. Stud fees, veterinary services, kennel facilities, equipment and food are essentials. Personal responsibilities include daily care of the dogs and maintenance of the kennel facility.

Preparation for becoming a breeder should include a secure knowledge of the breed standard, and an understanding of pedigrees. The concepts of linebreeding, inbreeding and outcrossing, and the study of dog anatomy, heredity and reproduction are necessary. The future breeder should also have a working knowledge of canine health, nutrition and first aid.

Unfortunately, there is no formal training provided for the breeder. Each will have to seek knowledge and gain experience through his own efforts. Read books, newsletters and magazines. Attend dog club meetings, seminars, clinics and lectures. Visit kennels, animal hospitals, training classes and dog shows. Investigate the curriculum at the nearest college or university for courses which might help you.

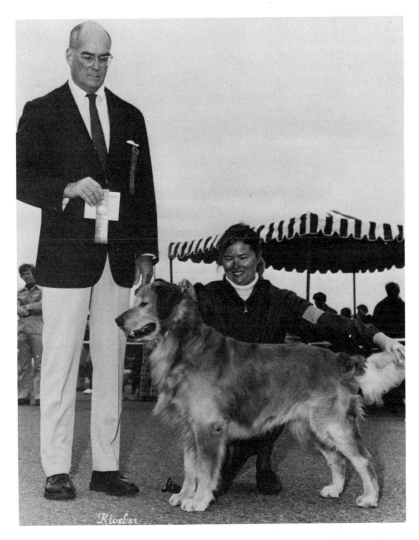

Nancy Kelly Belsaas, Westminster 1958, is a highly successful breeder of Golden Retrievers. She insists that her dogs be capable in field and obedience as well as proving themselves in the show ring. Nancy's long and varied experience includes JS, all-breed handler's assistant, apprentice handler, kennel manager, obedience trainer, owner of grooming and boarding business, veterinarian's assistant and handling instructor.

Joseph Sayres
New York
Irish Terriers.
Westminster JS winner in 1935 under the late famous professional handler and all-breed judge, Percy Roberts. A veterinarian in Buffalo for thirty years, Dr. Sayres breeds Irish Terriers and is working for approval as a judge for this breed.

10/Junior "Hall of Fame"

THIS chapter is a salute to the winners of Junior Showmanship over the years. The juniors pictured here represent the finest competitors and handlers in the United States and Canada. You will see juniors from all over the country handling a great variety of breeds of dogs. Some are Westminster Junior Showmanship winners, some are High-Score Junior Showmanship winners, and several are noted for their achievement in breed handling. You will learn that many of these juniors are still active in the dog world. They are breeders, handlers, judges, kennel owners and managers and some are even the parents of today's junior showmen.

The photographs we have chosen to use in this chapter have been selected to show the junior champions from many different breeds and parts of the country. We know that there are many noteworthy juniors not included. We also regret that there were some juniors whom we were unable to reach.

The caption information represents highlights of each junior's accomplishments and some of the breeds they have handled.

Betsy Long Burr
Long Island, N.Y.
Collies.
First place winner at Westminster's Children's Handling class, 1941. Sorry, no photo available.

Dorothy Long Hale
Long Island, N.Y.
Collies.
Junior Handling winner at Westbury Kennel Club, 1936. Best Obedience Handler at Westchester KC while still a junior, 1939.

Dorothy Long
Betsy Long

William P. Gilbert
Flemington, N.J.
Great Danes.
Competitor in Children's Handling, Westminster, 1942; Assistant Handler's license, 1946; Professional Handler's license, 1955. From leash to lens—now an official dog show photographer. Bill is pictured handling to Best in Show at Lancaster KC, 1964.

Patricia Detmold
Glen Garner, N.J.
English and Gordon Setters, Brittany Spaniels, English Cocker Spaniels.
Children's Handling wins included: Berwick, Nova Scotia, 1944; Halifax, Nova Scotia, 1945; Montreal, Quebec, 1946. Patricia bred and trained many champions, as well as dogs for Field and Obedience. Now a dog artist.

Barbara Worcester Keenan
Montclair, N.J.
West Highland White Terriers, Fox Terriers, and Scottish Terriers.
Barbara is picture with her first Westie, who later became Ch. Edgerstoune Cindy, foundation bitch of Wishing Well Kennels, home of 40 champions with wins of 50 Bests in Show. Top win, Best in Show with Westie, Ch. Elfinbrook Simon, at Westminster KC, 1962. Now a judge.

110

Lydia Coleman Hutchinson
Westport, Conn.
Cairn Terriers and Toy Poodles.
Lydia is pictured at age 11 with the first
dog she made a champion, Cairn Terrier
Ch. Shagbark Misty Betts. Lydia scored 15
Junior Showmanship wins between 1949
and 1954. They included: Second at West-
minster KC Junior Showmanship; First at
First Company Governor's Footguard Ath-
letic Assn.; First at Eastern DC, Boston.
Her Ch. Bonnie Bairn of Wolfpit was top
Cairn bitch in the U.S. for 1955–57, and
her Miniature Poodle, Ch. Hollycourt
Merry Spirit was Winners Bitch at West-
minster in 1955. Now a judge.

Betty Kemp Crossman
Greenville, R.I.
English and Gordon Setters.
Junior Showmanship wins include: First at Montpelier,
Vt.; First at Champlain Valley KC; First at Providence
County KC; and First at First Company Governor's
Footguard Athletic Assn. at Hartford. Betty finished
two Gordon Setters to championships.

**Marsha Hall Brown,
Greenville, R.I.**
English Setters, Irish Setters,
Gordon Setters, Beagles, Bas-
sets and Collies.

Marsha, co-author of this
book, is pictured at first Junior
Showmanship win at Willi-
mantic, Conn. 1950. Her Junior Showmanship Firsts included: Providence County
KC, Eastern Dog Club at Boston; First Company Gover-
nor's Footguard Athletic Assn.
at Hartford; Framingham KC.
Winner of the Gaines Youth
Aware, 1955. Marsha has bred
and handled English Setters to
championships, has been a licensed handler, vice-president
of the English Setter Assn. for
five years, and is a judge.

**George Alston,
Pasadena, Md.**
Winner of Westminster Junior Show-
manship, 1954. Now a licensed handler,
George and his wife, Mary Ann, own
Fieldstone Kennels, offering facilities
for boarding, grooming and training.
Specializing in Poodles and Sporting
dogs.

Patricia Leary LeMoigne
Pottersville, N.J.
Afghan Hound.
Pictured winning Westminster Kennel Club Junior Showmanship in 1956. Best of Breed at Afghan Hound Club of America Specialty at New York.

Ray Sumida
Monterey, Calif.
Irish Setters and English Setters.
Ray, the California Junior Handler of the Year in 1954, is an experienced handler of over 20 breeds. Pictured scoring Junior Championship win at Oakland, he was also Best Junior Showman at Golden Gate, 1956. Member, California Professional Handlers Assn.

Patricia Matson Alston
Long Island, N.Y.
English Springer Spaniels
Junior Showmanship winner at Westminster
KC, 1957. Now a professional handler.

Robert Harris
Long Island, N.Y.
Boxers, Beagles.
Second at Westminister KC Junior Showmanship, 1957. Stewards
Club of America, Top Boy Handler 1956–1957.

Bethny Hall Mason
Greenville, R.I.
English, Irish, and Gordon Setters, Afghans, Pointers, Beagles and Schipperkes.
Winner of Westminster KC Junior Showmanship, 1959; third at Westminster, 1956, '57; Best Junior Showman at First Company Governor's Footguard Athletic Assn. at Hartford, 1958; First at Eastern Dog Club, Boston, 1955, '56; Stewards Club of America, Top Girl Handler 1956, '57, and '58. Gaines Youth Award, 1959. Junior columnist for *Popular Dogs*. Now a judge.

**Nancy Kelly Belsaas
Stamford, Conn.**
Golden Retrievers, Collie, Poodles, Hounds and Toys.
First at Westminster, 1958; Gaines Youth Award Honorable Mention 1957; Licensed Assistant Handler; Obedience Trainer. Now a breeder of Goldens.

**Charlotte Martin Stacy
Virginia Beach, Va.**
Cocker Spaniels.
Junior Showmanship wins included First at Eastern Dog Club, Boston, and third at Westminster, 1958. Charlotte is pictured handling Ch. Bo-Art's Back Talk to Best in Show at Lewiston-Auburn KC, 1959. She is now a professional handler, together with her husband, W. Terry Stacy, specializing in Cocker Spaniels. Also an Obedience trainer.

116

**Jean Owen Parkhurst
Southington, Conn.**
English Setters, Pointers, Dachshunds.
Pictured in win of Best Junior Showman at First Company Governor's Footguard Athletic Assn. at Hartford, Conn., 1960. Also Junior Showmanship winner at Elm City KC at New Haven, and at Great Barrington, Mass. Junior showmanship finalist at Westminster in 1959, '60 and '61. Jean trained and handled several English Setters to their championships.

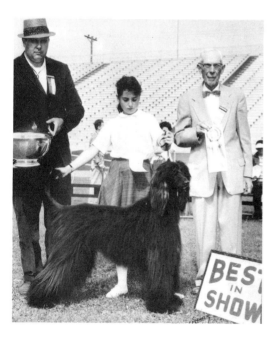

**Jennifer Sheldon
Massapequa, N.Y.**
Afghan Hounds.
First in Junior Showmanship at Westminster in 1965, after having been Second in 1962, '63 and '64. Pictured handling to all-breed Best in Show at Scranton, Pa., she also went BIS with her Afghan at Devon, Pa. Handled Afghan to Best of Opposite Sex win at Westminster, two years, and Rottweiler to Best in Specialty at Trenton.

117

Anna Maria Stimmler Burke
Fairview Village, Pa.
Maltese and Poodles.
Obedience award winner, 1958.
Winner of High Score Trophy for
most Junior Showmanship wins in
1962 (awarded in 1963). Best Junior
Showman at First Company
Governor's Footguard Athletic
Assn. at Hartford, 1963. Third in
JS at Westminster, 1963. Handled
Maltese, Ch. Co-Ca-He's
Aennchen Toy Dancer to First in
Toy Group at Westminster, 1964.
Scored 8 Bests in Show and 24
Firsts in Toy Group with her Maltese.

Clare Hodge
Bryn Mawr, Pa.
Whippets.
Winner of Junior Showmanship at
Westminster, 1964.

118

William Coleman
Durham, N.C.
Beagles.
Breeder of four litters of Beagles. Winner of five First in Junior Showmanship, including pictured win at Vineland, N.J., 1964. A judge.

Ann Bowley
Woodruff Collies
Durham, N.H.
Collies, Briards.
Best Junior Handler, Collie Club of N.H. 1965; National 4-H Dog Care and Training Champion award winner, 1964; Junior Handling 4-H State Champion, 1963 and 1965. Handled Collies to wins of Winners Bitch and Best of Opposite Sex at Westminster, 1966, '67, '68 and '70. Winners Bitch with Briard, 1969. A professional handler.

Left:
Richard Van Istendal
Hatboro, Pa.
Keeshonden and Scottish Terriers.
First winner of Novice and Open at Valley Forge KC Junior Showmanship. Finalist in Westminster JS, 1966.

Right:
Edward Van Istendal
Hatboro, Pa.
Keeshonden and Scottish Terriers.
Recipient of the George F. Foley Educational Trust Award, 1970–71 (Penn State University). Finalist in Westminster KC Junior Showmanship, 1964, '65 and '66.

Above:
Deborah Duguid
Toronto, Ont., Canada
Airedale Terriers.
Best Junior Handler at Syracuse, N.Y.
Won three consecutive JS championships
at Ottawa, 1965, '66 and '67 to gain perma-
nent possession of Doris Courtney Trophy.
(Pictured in 1966 win.) JS winner at Cha-
grin Valley KC, Ohio, for two years, and a
finalist at Detroit for two years.

At left:
Melody Stoltz
Sun Valley, Calif.
Toy Poodles, Boston Terriers, Italian Grey-
hounds, Yorkshire Terriers, Lhasa Apsos,
Shih Tzus, and Welsh Terriers.
Best Western Junior Handler, 1969. First
in JS at Beverly Hills KC, 1968. Finalist in
Westminster KC Junior Showmanship,
1969.

121

Linda Young
West Newbury, Mass.
Irish Setters, Boxers, Harriers, Dachshunds, and Cockers.
Junior Showmanship wins include: First at South Shore KC, 1956; First at Springfield KC, 1967; First at Champlain Valley KC, 1966, '67; and Second at Westminster KC, 1967. Handled Winners Dog Irish at Combined Setter Specialty in New York, 1968.

David Lynn Brumbaugh
Perry, Georgia
Pomeranians, Labrador Retrievers, Miniature Schnauzers.
Pictured scoring First in Junior Showmanship at Westminster KC, 1967. David owns and breeds Miniature Schnauzers.

Laurel Howe Stone
Westfield, N.J.
English Setters.
Junior of the Year, Hudson
English Setter Club,
1965–1969. Winner of the English Setter Association of
America Junior Showman
Award for 1965, '66, '67 and
'68, and runner-up in 1969.
Winner of 24 Junior High
Score awards. A professional
handler.

Cody Sickle
Evanston, Ill.
Bulldog
Finalist in Westminster KC
Junior Showmanship. Pictured
winning Best in Show with
Ch. Cherokee Morgan at Mid-
Hudson KC in 1969.

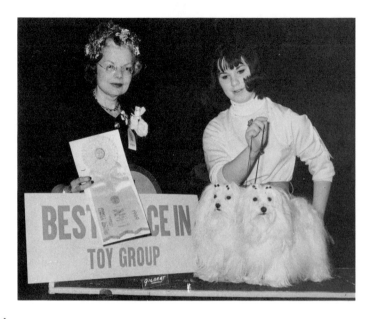

Above:
Daryl Martin
Highland Park, Ill.
Lhasa Apsos, Maltese and Shih Tzus.
Pictured handling Maltese to Best Brace in Toy Group at Westminster 1969 under judge Anna Katherine Nicholas. Twice winner of First in Toy Group at International KC at Chicago. Daryl has won 15 Bests in Show and 25 Group Firsts with her Maltese, Ch. Martin's Jingles Puff and Ch. Martin's Bangles Puff. A professional handler.

At right:
Susan Gilman
Nashua, N.H.
Whippets.
First win at Maryland KC, 1964. Winner of High Score Trophy for 1965 and 1967. Second, Westminster Kennel Club Junior Showmanship, 1970.

Top:
Kimberly Haigler
Fullerton, California
Irish Setters, English Springer Spaniels, Australian Terriers.
Winner of 13 Firsts in Junior Showmanship. Winner, Irish Setter Club of America Annual Junior Award, 1968 and 1969. Pictured with Ch. Michael's Patty O'Shea, Best of Breed and Group third at Sacramento, Calif.

At right:
Melissa Beth Brumbaugh
Perry, Georgia
Miniature Schnauzers, Maltese, Pomeranians and Labrador Retrievers.
Junior Showmanship wins include Miami, Fort Worth, and Memphis. Pictured winning Toy Group with Maltese at Macon, Ga. 1970 under judge Haskell Schuffman.

125

**Heidi Shellenbarger
Costa Mesa, California**
Whippets, German Shorthaired Pointers, English Cocker Spaniels and Cairn Terriers.

Junior Showmanship Firsts at Ventura Dog Fanciers, 1970; Beverly Hills KC, 1970; and Westminster KC, 1971. Heidi put major points on Ch. Gretchenhof Newporter with Winners Dog win at Sir Frances Drake KC, and was Best of Opposite Sex with the Whippet, Ch. Gretchenhof Sea Witch at Orange Empire KC.

**Charles A. Westfield III
Huntington, N.Y.**
Bulldogs and Chows.

Junior Showmanship wins include First at Eastern Dog Club, 1968, and Thirds at Westminster KC, 1970 and 1971. Has handled Bulldogs to wins of Bulldog Club of Connecticut Specialty 1970, and breed and Group third at Mid-Hudson KC. Handled Chow in win of Best of Breed (3-pt. major) from puppy class at Burlington County KC, 1968. University of Purdue graduate 1977 in Biochemistry and Animal Science. Now in graduate school for Veterinarian Medicine.

126

Holly Howe
Chester, New Jersey
English Setters, Gordon Setters, Pointers, Afghan Hounds.
Qualified for Westminster 1969, 1971 and 1972. Finalist 1972. One of the Top Five Junior Handlers in the Nation in 1972. Junior Handling Award and Junior Showmanship Top Open Senior for English Setter Association of America 1971 and 1972. Best Junior Handler at Penn Ridge Kennel Club and Rockland County Kennel Club 1972. Winner of the Trenton Kennel Club Annual Trophy 1972. Breed wins include several finished champions, numerous Bests of Breed and Two Group firsts.

Alison Stockland
Santa Ana, California
German Shorthaired Pointers, Labrador Retrievers, Irish Setters.
Qualified for Westminster 1972, 22 Open firsts, 13 Best Junior Showman Awards, Best of Breed at San Antonio National Specialty. Finished her Shorthaired with a 5 point major.

127

Pamela Brink
Culver City, California
Dalmatians and Whippets.
Qualified for Westminster
1973 and 1974. Best Junior in
the U.S. with a Dalmatian
1972 and 1973. Active in
breed, JS and Obedience. Finished her Dalmatian. Panel
member at California JS Semi-
nar. Handling instructor. Junior Showmanship judge.

Claudia Weniger
Santa Barbara, California
English and Irish Setters.
Qualified for Westminster 1974 and 1975. Top winning California Junior
Handler 1975. Finished English and Irish Setters. Handler assistant.

128

**Virginia Westfield
Huntington, New York**
Bulldogs, Great Danes,
Chow Chows, Irish Water
Spaniels.
Westminster winner 1975.
First Company Governor's
Footguard Trophy 1969.
Best Junior Handler at
Westchester Kennel Club,
Eastern Dog Club, West-
bury Kennel Club, Bucks
County Kennel Club,
Maryland Kennel Club,
Worcester Kennel Club,
Bryn Mawr Kennel Club,
and Middlesex Kennel
Club. Breeder-owner of
two Best in Show Bulldogs.
Now a licensed Junior
Showmanship Judge.

**Jordan Gray Freeauf
Macon, Georgia**
English and Irish Setters.
Qualified for Westminster 1974–1976. Top Junior Award from Irish Setter
Club of America and Irish Setter Club of Georgia 1974 and 1975. Handler
assistant.

129

Lisa Swanson
Woodinville, Washington
Weimaraners.
Qualified for Westminster in 1975 and 1976. Best Northwest Junior Handler 1976. Weimaraner Club of America Junior Award Runner-Up, 1976 and 1977. Finished Weimaraners in breed and Obedience with Group placements in US and Canada.

Doug Belter
Edmonton, Alberta, Canada
English and Irish Setters, English Bulldog.
Junior Showmanship Top Senior Handler in Alberta 1974–1975, Best Junior Handler Overall, Crambrook, British Columbia 1975, Best Junior Handler overall in Manitoba at Northwinds 1975, Best In Show, top English Setter in Canada and Top Ten Sporting in Canada 1976. Finished his English Setter in U.S.A. by taking WD and BW at the National Specialty, the Golden Gate Setter Specialty and The Far West Setter Specialty.

Lisa Kalmbrum
Napa, California
Samoyeds and breeds
from each group.
15 Best Junior Handler
Awards in the U.S. and Canada. Finished three Samoyeds,
bred two champions. BOB at
Santa Clara 1975 and Reno
1977. Assistant Handler.

Diane Lynne Haywood
Palos Verdes, California
Dalmatians, Cairn Terriers.
Qualified for Westminster
1975. Nine JS firsts in 1975,
High Scoring Junior Handler in Obedience 1975,
Best Junior Handler in California 1976, Best Junior
handling a Dalmatian in
U.S. 1976. Finished her
Dalmatian with three BOB.
One Cairn to title.

131

Randy McAteer
Ocala, Florida
Irish Setters, Bulldogs, Welsh
Corgis, Maltese, Miniature
Wirehaired Dachshunds.

Westminster Winner 1977. Named Best Junior Handler by the Irish Setter Club of Amer
Greater Miami Dog Club and Irish Setter Club of Georgia 1977. Twenty-two wins in O
JS. Breed wins include finishing three champions and BOB and Group 3 with a Dalmati

Donald Sturz, Jr.
Huntington, New York
Golden Retrievers, Poodles
Borzoi, Whippets, Smooth
Terrier.

Qualified for Westminster 1972–1978 and was finalist twice. High Score Award 1975
1977. Named Top Junior Handler by *Kennel Review* and Owner Handler Association. H
dled the number 1 Golden Retriever Bitch in the U.S. in 1977. Columnist for *Ken
Review*.

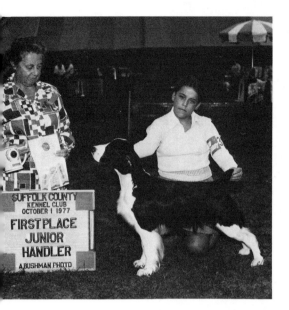

Lisa Jane Alston
Remsemburg, New York
English Springer Spaniels, Whippets, Irish Setters, Longhaired Dachshunds. Westminster finalist 1972 and 1973. Best Junior Handler at Rockland County and Suffolk County. Many breed wins including a Group 4 with a Lakeland Terrier.

Lisa's parents are Westminster winners George Alston and Pat Matson Alston.

Taffe Walker
Delta, British Columbia
English and Irish Setters.

Westminster finalist 1978. English Setter Association of America, Canadian Junior Award 1972–1977. Best Junior Handler in Alberta 1973, Vancouver Junior Kennel Club Trophy 1973. Best in Show in Edmonton 1974 with her English Setter and Best in Show in Bermuda with her Irish Setter, WB at the California English Setter Club in 1976 with her Fantails Mandarin Orange.

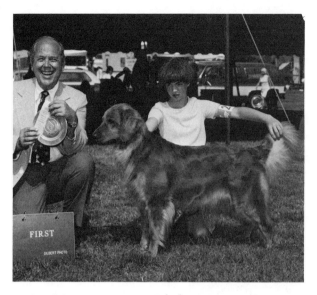

Janet Sturz
Huntington, New York
Golden Retrievers and
German Wirehaired Pointe

Qualified for Westminster 1975–1977. Metropolitan New York's Top Junior 1976, *Kennel Review* Top Open Junior 1977. President of Long Island Junior Handlers Club. Handled her Pointer to championship with BOB wins.

Stacey Martin
Old Tappan, New Jersey
Standard Schnauzer,
Lhasa Apso,
Miniature Schnauzers.

Qualified for Westminster 1978. National Schnauzer Club America Junior Handler of the Year. Successful in breed and Raises, trains and handles her own dogs. Match show judge.

134

Laura Mazzaro
Huntington, Conn.
Norwegian Elkhounds.
Qualified for Westminster 1974–1978, finalist 1974, 1976 and 1978. Firsts at Eastern Dog Club, Elm City and the Connecticut State Junior Trophy 1974–1976. Handled her Elkhound to top 10 in breed and finished Canadian Championship.

Heidi Martin
Libertyville, Illinois
Basset Hounds and Pembroke Welsh Corgi.
Qualified for Westminster 1975–1978, finalist in 1977. Best Junior Handler at Detroit 1976, International 1975, Top Junior Handler for Basset Hound Club of America 1975 and 1976 and State of Illinois 1976. Breed wins include two champions and several BOB's.

135

Lee Langley Freeauf
Macon, Georgia
Irish and English Setters, Basenji,
German Shorthaired Pointer.
Qualified for Westminster 1976–1978. Irish
Setter Club of Georgia Top Junior 1976. Finished two Basenji, several BOB wins with
Group 2.

Dionne Butt
Honey Brook, Pennsylvania
Whippets, Deerhounds, Greyhounds
and English Cocker Spaniels.
Qualified for Westminster 1972–1978. Finalist four times with placements of third
and fourth. Winner of the *Kennel Review*
Winkie three years in a row and *Dog
World* Award. She has Thirty-two group
placements with five group firsts and three
Bests in Show. Finished eight Deerhounds, one Greyhound, 17 Whippets and
one English Cocker Spaniel. Total wins in
JS from 1972–1978 are about 100.

136

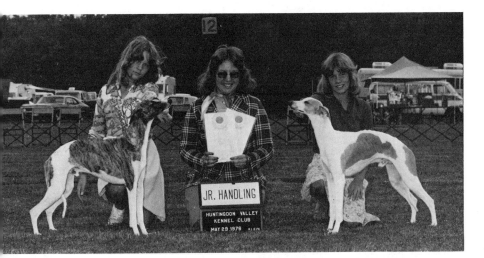

Left:
Jennifer Butt
Honey Brook, Pa.
Whippets and English
Cocker Spaniel.
Qualified for Westminster three times.
Westminster third in 1977. Winner of the
Kennel Review Winkie in 1975. Breed wins
include finishing four Whippets and one
English Cocker. Two group placements
with her Whippets. Total wins in JS are 45.

Right:
Melissa Butt
Honey Brook, Pa.
Whippets, Deerhounds
and Greyhounds.
Winner of the *Kennel Review* Winkie in
1976. She has finished four Whippets, one
Greyhound and one Deerhound. One
group placement. Total JS wins are 67.

Susan Schneider
Lorton, Virginia
Kerry Blue Terriers,
English Springer Spaniels, Vizsla,
Bullmastiff, Keeshonds.
Qualified for Westminster 1973–1978, fi-
nalist 1978. Best Junior Handler at Langley
Kennel Club 1974 and 1975, Harrisburg
1977, and Chagrin Valley 1977. 48 firsts in
Open JS. Finished three champions and
won BOS at the Kerry Blue National Spe-
cialty. Six group placements. Handlers as-
sistant.

Anne Greene
Avon, Connecticut
English Setters.
Qualified for Westminster 1978. Be
Junior Handler at Farmington Valle
1975, Open Senior First at Con
bined Setter Specialty 1978. Succe
in breed includes 16 BOS in 197
and 1977 and BOS in 1978 at Con
bined Setter Specialty.

Sonda Peterson
San Diego, California
Boxers, Rottweilers, Great Danes, Boston Terriers. Westminster Winner
1978.

138

11/Junior Crowns

JUNIORS wear many crowns. In this section you will find a list of these special awards and titles and a short description of the competitions.

Westminster Junior Showmanship Champion
(The Leonard Brumby Sr. Memorial Trophy)

The JS competition held at the Westminster Kennel Club show at New York's Madison Square Garden is limited to Juniors who have won eight Open Division firsts at dog shows held under AKC rules where championship points are awarded.

For many years this competition consisted of one class of winning juniors, judged by one licensed professional handler. The first place winner was named top junior of the year.

This competition is now held in four sections. Two different judges preside over these classes. Two classes are judged on Monday and two classes are judged on Tuesday. Two juniors are selected from each of these classes to compete in the finals. A third judge presides over the competition of the eight finalists and names a winner, a second, a third, and a fourth.

Top Southern Junior Handler

In 1970 the first regional competition was held for juniors in the Southern states. Juniors who reside in the following states are eligible to qualify: Alabama, Arkansas, Florida, Georgia, Louisiana, Mississippi, North Carolina, Oklahoma, South Carolina, Tennessee and Texas. One first place in the Open JS class at a participating kennel club show qualifies for this annual competition. The competition is held each year at different Southern shows and consists of two preliminary classes and a final competition.

Dog Writer's Association of America Annual Trophy

Awarded to the Junior who demonstrates the most Sportsmanship at dog shows. It is awarded in memory of Wentzle Ruml Jr. The Junior who receives the most number of votes wins this trophy.

Top Rocky Mountain Junior Handler

The first annual competition for juniors who reside in the following states was held in 1972: Arizona, Colorado, Idaho, Kansas, Montana, Nebraska, New Mexico, North Dakota, South Dakota, Utah and Wyoming. One win in the Open JS class at a participating kennel club show qualifies a junior for the competition to be held at shows in the eleven state area.

Kennel Club of Beverly Hills Junior Championship
Los Angeles, California.

The Harry Sangster Memorial Trophy is awarded to the winner of the annual junior championship competition held in conjunction with the Beverly Hills Kennel Club's summer show. Juniors must have won at least one Open JS class during the year to qualify for this annual competition.

First Company Governor's Footguard Athletic Association
Hartford, Conn.

The Governor of the State of Connecticut offers the trophy to the junior judged Best Junior Showman at the Hartford show JS competition each year. The winners of the JS classes at this show compete for the Governor's Trophy.

International Kennel Club
Chicago, Ill.

The JS competition at Chicago is one of the largest in the country. This coveted win is the goal of many top junior showmen.

Ottawa Championship Show, Ottawa, Ontario, Canada

This Doris Courtney Trophy is awarded to the top winning junior showman in the JS classes each year. A junior must win this award three times to gain permanent possession of the trophy.

The Annual High Score Award

Each year the Annual High Score Trophy is presented by *Dog World* to the junior who wins the most number of JS firsts during the year.

Ray Sumida, California Junior of the Year, 1954.

Christine Pulscher, Houston, Texas. Winner of the first Top Southern Junior Handler Award 1969. Chris handled her Basenji to the top spot at Shreveport, La., 1970.

Anna Maria Stimmler Burke, Fairview Village, Pa., receiving trophy from Governor John Dempsey for Best Junior Handler at Hartford, Conn. 1963.

Owner Handler Association of America Annual Trophy

Awarded to the Junior who has the highest number of points in the Junior classes.

Starved Rock Kennel Club High Score Award

Awarded to the Junior from Illinois who has the greatest number of Junior wins.

Trenton Kennel Club Annual Trophy

Awarded to the high scoring Junior from New Jersey.

Connecticut Trophy

Awarded annually to the Junior from Connecticut with the greatest number of Junior wins.

Top Mid-Atlantic Junior Handler

Tidewater Kennel Club of Virginia's all breed show holds this Limited Junior Showmanship class. The juniors competing must be from New Jersey, Pennsylvania, Delaware, Maryland, Ohio, Kentucky, West Virginia, Virginia or North Carolina. To qualify, a junior must have won first place in one or more open classes at an AKC licensed or member show.

Alaskan Top Junior Handler Plaque

Annual award given to the Junior handler who has received the highest number of points for wins in JS competition at shows held in Alaska. This plaque is given each year at the club's annual awards banquet.

Best California Junior Handler

Limited Classes are held annually at the Sun Maid KC show. Two Open Class wins are needed to qualify.

Best Northwest Junior Handler

Federation Provincial Junior Handling Championships

A limited or championship JS competition is held in most of the provinces of Canada each year. Rules differ according to the Federation of Dog Clubs in the province.

Annual Breed Club Awards

Many breed clubs offer awards to junior members for achievement in JS. Information concerning these awards should be requested from the club secretary or awards chairman. (The English Setter Association of America was one of the first to sponsor annual junior awards and at present offers trophies for JS, breed handling, Obedience and Field.)

Dog Writers' Association of America

Annual contest open to all writers. Junior writers under 18 years of age are invited to submit entries. This is an annual competition judged on outstanding writing ability about dogs.

The following three awards, listed for the record, are no longer offered:

*Champion Junior Handler of California, Oakland, Calif.
*The Stewards Club of America Award
*The Gaines Youth Award

Westminster Kennel Club Junior Winners

1933   First Children's Handling winner not recorded.
1934   Winner not recorded.
1935   Joseph Sayres—Irish Terrier.
1936   Dorothea McAnulty.
1937   Winner not recorded.
1938   Arthur Mulvihill, N.Y.
1939   Mona Saphir—Ol English Sheepog.
1940   Jerry Werber, N.Y.
1941   Betsy Long, N.Y.—Collie.
1942   Betty Hinks
1943   Walter Wilson—Gordon Setter.
1944   Betty Bolger, Pa.
1945   Evelyn Staubmueller
1946   Frank Hill, Pa.
1947   John Herr, Lancaster, Pa.
1948   George Metz, N.Y.—Boston Terrier.
1949   Monica Rumpf, N.Y.
1950   Hope Johnson, West Hartford, Conn.
1951   Theodore Hallender, Mass.
1952   William Henry.
1953   Phyllis Campbell, Rhode Island—Great Dane.
1954   George Alston, Pa.—Boxer.
1955   Mary Donnelly, N.J.—Irish Terrier.
1956   Patricia Leary, N.J.—Afghan.
1957   Patricia Matson, N.Y.—Springer Spaniel.
1958   Nancy Kelly, Conn.—Golden Retriever.
1959   Bethny Hall, R.I.—Irish Setter.
1960   Allen Kirk, Va.—Scottish Terrier.
1961   Betty Lou Ham, Mass.—Irish Setter.
1962   Susan Heckmann, Maryland—Dachshund.
1963   Lydia Ceccarine, N.Y.—Boxer.
1964   Clare Hodge, Pa.—Whippet.
1965   Jennifer Sheldon, N.Y.—Afghan.
1966   Laura Swyler, N.Y.—Wire-haired Dachshund.
1967   David Lynn Brumbaugh, Ga.—Miniature Schnauzer.
1968   Cheryl Baker, Mass.—Pointer.
1969   Charles Garvin, Ohio—Dalmatian.
1970   Patricia Hardy, Ohio—Golden Retriever.
1971   Heidi Shellenbarger, Calif.—Whippet.
1972   Deborah Von Ahrens, New Jersey—Afghan Hound.
1973   Teresa Nail—Doberman Pinscher.
1974   Leslie Church, Missouri—Miniature Schnauzer.
1975   Virginia Westfield, New York—Bulldog.
1976   Kathy Hritzo, Ohio—Samoyed.
1977   Randy McAteer, Florida—Irish Setter.
1978   Sonda Peterson, California—Boxer.

12/ AKC Regulations for Junior Showmanship

(Effective July 9, 1980)

Note: These regulations implement the following dog show rule:

A Club or Association holding a show may offer Junior Showmanship if it so chooses. The classes and procedure shall conform to the American Kennel Club regulations governing Junior Showmanship, as adopted by the Board of Directors.

Section 1. **Approval of Classes.** Any club that is approved to hold a licensed or member all-breed show or a specialty show held apart from an all-breed show, may also be approved to offer Junior Showmanship competition at its show.

Section 2. **Standard for Judging.** Junior Showmanship shall be judged solely on the ability and skill of the Juniors in handling their dogs as in the breed ring. The show qualities of the dogs shall not be considered. Junior handlers shall not be required to exchange dogs. The judge must excuse a handler and dog from the ring if, in his opinion, the handler cannot properly control the dog.

Section 3. **Approval of Judges.** Any person who is eligible to be approved to judge one or more breeds at AKC licensed or member shows and any person who has filed a special judging application which has been approved by the Board of Directors, may be approved to judge Junior Showmanship.

The name and assignment of each judge shall be included in the list of judges sent to AKC for approval. Junior Showmanship entries shall be included in computing judges' assignments under Chapter 10, Section 13 of the Dog Show Rules.

A judge will not be disapproved for a Junior Showmanship assignment because of its proximity in time and distance to another Junior Showmanship assignment. Any change in judges shall be handled in accordance with the Dog Show Rules.

Section 4. **Classes and Divisions.** The regular Junior Showmanship classes shall be:

(A) *Novice.* This class shall be for boys and girls who are at least 10 years old and under 17 years old on the day of the show and who, at the time entries close, have not won more than 3 first place awards in a Novice class at a licensed or member show.

(B) *Open.* This class shall be for boys and girls who are at least 10 years old and under 17 years old on the day of the show, and who have won 3 first place awards in a Novice Junior Showmanship Class at a licensed or member show. The winner of a Novice class shall automatically become eligible to enter and to compete in the Open class at the same show provided that the win is his 3rd first place award in Novice and provided that there are one or more Junior Handlers competing in Open Class.

Junior handlers who win a third Novice Class after the closing of entries for a show may transfer their entry from the Novice Class to the Open Class provided that this transfer is made by the Superintendent or Show Secretary prior to the start of judging at the show.

(C) *Junior and Senior Classes.* Either or both of these regular classes may be divided by age into Junior and Senior classes, provided the division is specified in the premium list. A Junior class shall be for boys and girls who are at least 10 years old and under 13 years old on the day of the show. A Senior class shall be for boys and girls who are at least 13 years old and under 17 years old on the day of the show.

(D) *Classes for Boys and Girls.* Any or all of these regular classes may also be divided by sex to provide a class or classes for Boys and a class or classes for Girls, provided the division is specified in the premium list.

(E) *Best Junior Handler.* A club offering Junior Showmanship may offer a prize for Best Junior Handler provided the prize is offered in the premium list. The Junior handler placed first in each of the regular Junior Showmanship classes, if undefeated in any other Junior Showmanship class at that show, shall automatically be eligible to compete for this prize.

Section 5. **Armbands.** Armbands with the catalog numbers of the dogs shall be worn by the Junior handlers.

Section 6. **Eligibility of Dog.** Each dog handled in a regular Junior Showmanship class must be entered and shown in one of the breed or obedience classes at the show, or must be entered for Junior Showmanship only. Each dog must be owned or co-owned by the Junior handler or by the Junior handler's father, mother, brother, sister, uncle, aunt, grandfather or grandmother, including the corresponding step and half relations. Every dog entered for Junior Showmanship must be eligible to compete in Dog Shows or in Obedience trials. At a Specialty show, each dog must be of the breed for which the show is held.

A dog that has been excused or disqualified by a breed judge or by a Bench

146

Show Committee may still be handled in Junior Showmanship if eligible to compete in Obedience trials. A dog that has been rejected, dismissed or excused by the veterinarian for the protection of the other dogs at the show or for the protection of the dog excused, may not be handled in Junior Showmanship.

Section 7. **Premium List.** A club that has been approved to offer Junior Showmanship must list the classification in its premium list, with a description of the entry requirements for each class offered, and the name of the judge of each class. The number of entries in any or all classes may be limited, provided the limits are specified in the premium list.

Section 8. **Entry Forms.** To be acceptable each entry form must meet all of the requirements of Chapter 15, Section 4 of the Dog Show Rules and must show in the appropriate areas the name and address of the Junior Handler, the Class which the Junior Handler is entering, the Junior Handler's date of birth, and if the dog is not owned or co-owned by the Junior handler, his relationship to the owner. The identification slip for the entry of the dog shall show the entry in Junior Showmanship and the class.

Section 9. **Closing of Entries.** Entries for regular Junior Showmanship classes shall close at the same time that entries close for the show.

Section 10. **Judging Program.** The judging program shall list the Junior Showmanship classes, the ring(s) in which they are to be judged, the name(s) of the judge(s), the hour of judging, and the number of entries in each class.

Section 11. **Catalog.** The information on any dog entered for Junior Showmanship only shall be listed at the end of the listing of its breed or variety. The dog's catalog number, the breed, and the name of the Junior handler shall be listed by classes under a separate section for Junior Showmanship.

Section 12. **Ribbons and Prizes.** The color of ribbons or rosettes for Junior Showmanship classes shall be:
    First Prize — Rose
    Second Prize — Brown
    Third Prize — Light Green
    Fourth Prize — Gray
They shall be at least 2 inches wide and approximately 8 inches long, and shall bear a facsimile of the AKC seal, the words Junior Showmanship, the name of the show-giving club, and the date.
No money prizes shall be offered. All other prizes must be described or value stated, and must be offered for outright award. No prize may be offered that is conditional upon the breed of the dog being handled.

Section 13. Each club holding Junior Showmanship shall provide for the judge a judge's book, which shall contain a breed judging sheet with appropriate headings for each Junior Showmanship class. The judge shall place the handlers first, second, third and fourth, and mark his book accordingly. Absentees should be noted in the judge's book along with the dogs excused and the reason therefore. The judge should note the time that he commences, and the time that he finishes judging, and shall sign this book.

Section 14. **Limited Classes.** A club that is approved to hold a licensed or member all-breed show, may be approved to hold a Limited Junior Showmanship class or classes at its show, but no club will be approved to hold regular Junior Showmanship classes and Limited Junior Showmanship classes at the same show.

Limited Junior Showmanship classes shall be open only to Junior handlers who have qualified by reason of certain wins in Junior Showmanship competition as specified in the premium list, within a specified period of about 12 months ending not more than 3 months prior to the date of the show; and may be further limited to Junior handlers who reside within a specified geographical area, or who have qualified at shows held within a specified geographical area.

Section 15. **Exceptions for Limited Classes.** All of these Regulations relating to regular Junior Showmanship classes shall also apply to Limited Junior Showmanship classes except that:

(A) The club may choose to prepare an announcement, separate from the premium list, which shall give all of the required information on the Limited Junior Showmanship and which shall be distributed, on request, to eligible Junior handlers. Special entry forms, identification slips, and armbands, may also be provided, if necessary.

(B) The premium list or separate announcement may specify a closing date for acceptance of entries in Limited Junior Showmanship classes later than the date for closing of entries in the show.

(C) The dogs handled in Limited Junior Showmanship must be eligible for entry in Dog Shows or Obedience Trials. They may, but need not, be entered in breed or obedience at the particular show. Any limitation or restriction on entries in a show shall not apply to dogs that are brought into the show premises only to be handled in Limited Junior Showmanship.

(D) The information on dogs to be handled in Limited Junior Showmanship that are not entered in the show, and the names of the Junior handlers, may but need not be given in the catalog.

148

(E) The age limits specified in Section 4 shall apply to the age of each Junior handler at the time of the last win required to qualify for the Limited Junior Showmanship class, rather than to the age on the date of the Limited Junior Showmanship competition.

(F) If the entries in Limited Junior Showmanship warrant, the club may specify, in the first or in a later announcement, that preliminary classes will be held at the show, from which the judge(s) will select a specified number of Juniors to compete for Best Junior Handler, and no placements will be made in the preliminary classes.

(G) If, after the close of entries for a Limited Junior Showmanship competition, it develops that for any reason a dog to be handled in the competition cannot be shown, the Junior Handler may substitute another otherwise eligible dog, provided he supplies the Superintendent or Show Secretary with the required identifying information on the dog prior to the start of judging of the class in which the Junior Handler is to compete.

Section 16. **Records.** The Superintendent or Shows Secretary shall forward to the American Kennel Club, with the records of the show, the judge's books for the Junior Showmanship classes.

For those seeking further information, the address of the American Kennel Club is 51 Madison Avenue, New York, N.Y. 10010.

Bryan Martin, approved Junior Showmanship Judge. Former Junior Handler who qualified for Westminster 1967–71; finalist and third place in 1968. Bryan and his brother Peter are founders of the Junior Handlers Association which was organized in 1973 with help from the AKC and the PHA. Peter, the founding Treasurer of the JHA, is also an approved JS judge.

13/How to Judge Junior Showmanship

THIS chapter is written to instruct those who judge Junior Showmanship. It contains the judging standard, the qualifications and responsibilities of a judge and a step-by-step guide on judging procedure. There are tips on organizing the ring, an illustration of the judge's book and the new special feature—a judge's scorecard. Juniors, parents and stewards will also find helpful information for them.

The Standard for Judging

"Junior Showmanship shall be judged solely on the ability and skill of the Juniors in handling their dogs as in the breed ring. The show qualities of the dogs shall not be considered. Junior handlers shall not be required to exchange dogs. The judge must excuse a handler and dog from the ring if, in his opinion, the handler cannot properly control the dog." *Section 2 AKC Regulations for Junior Showmanship.*

Judges shall test the handling ability of each competitor. There are four basic areas for the judge to evaluate.

1. Handling skill and style appropriate to the breed. It is of primary importance that the judge select for merit those Juniors who handle their breed correctly.

2. Skills used to present the dog at its best. The judge must determine which Juniors are skilled in presenting their dogs' attributes and minimizing their dogs' faults.

3. Knowledge of ring procedures. The judge shall consider capable those juniors who follow directions, make appropriate turns and are aware of judging procedure.

4. Appearance and conduct. The judge shall consider important the Junior's appearance and conduct. Particular notice is to be made of suitable attire, proper grooming, manners and the Junior's regard for the dog.

Qualifications

Junior Showmanship judges must be judges who are eligible for one or more breeds or former Junior Showmanship competitors who are eligible to judge the JS classes.

These qualifications mean only that these are the judges who *may* officiate. The choice of a capable judge is more complex. JS judges must know the standard and the four basic areas for evaluation. They must have the experience necessary to make knowledgeable decisions. A JS judge should be genuinely interested in young people and regard the competition as a serious part of dog shows.

Some of the best JS judges are former all-breed handlers, former Junior Showmanship competitors and parents of successful competitors.

Responsibilities

A JS judge has specific responsibilities to the Juniors, the parents and to the show-giving club. The first consideration must be safety. Juniors with varying degrees of experience and dogs with great differences in size, temperament and training need safe ring conditions.

A responsible JS judge organizes the ring allowing each Junior sufficient space to pose and gait his or her dog. The judge may also request that the steward observe all classes with safety in mind. Any junior who can not control a dog or any disruptive dog must be excused.

Fair judging based on skill and ability is a judge's job. Previous wins, records, personal misfortunes or crowd appeal must never influence a decision. The judge is responsible for being prompt, prepared and courteous. The appearance of the judge should be an example for juniors to follow.

Preparations—Get Ready to Judge

Find out before judging what classes are scheduled and the number of entries in each class. Know what the judge's book looks like and what information you are required to fill in. Note that the class is marked in a box at the top. The age limits are marked in a box on the next line. You must also fill in the names of the juniors who place, their armband numbers and the breeds handled. Times of start and finish are at the bottom of the page with a blank for the number competing and the judge's signature.

Plan to use the scorecard and choose clothing with a pocket to carry it in.

Tell your stewards how they can help you. Request that all classes enter in catalog order. Show the steward where you want the examining table placed. Discuss your concern for safety in the ring. You may also ask the steward to record entry numbers and breed abbreviations on the scorecard sheets *before* the class enters the ring. This information is in the show catalog and is not available to judges before and during the class judging.

The Junior Showmanship Scorecard

Your skill as a judge comes from knowledge, experience, preparation, organization and common sense. Your performance as a judge depends on your ability to remember and sort numerous details. The JS scorecard is a simple system of recording these details.

Designed for judges by judges, the scorecard is a combination of special features which makes prompt, efficient, and ac-

JUNIOR SHOWMANSHIP COMPETITION

CATALOG NUMBER	AWARD	CATALOG NUMBER	AWARD	CATALOG NUMBER	AWARD	CATALOG NUMBER	AWARD	CATALOG NUMBER	AWARD
NOVICE JUNIOR		NOVICE SENIOR		OPEN JUNIOR		OPEN SENIOR			
5		(6)		22		41			
(6)		(8)		(35)		43			
(7)		(15)		(37)		(45)			
(9)		31		(39)		(47)			
(21)				(41)		(49)			
				(43)		(51)			
						(53)			
						55			

Sample page from the AKC Junior Showmanship Judge's book.

curate judging possible. It fits in an inside breast or side pocket of a man's coat or in the pocket of a woman's dress or jacket. The score sheets are adaptable to any size of class.

If the steward has not filled in the class, entry numbers and breed abbreviations before class time, the judge can easily record this information as the class enters the ring. The five basic categories cover all handling skills.

The simple rating system of a plus, minus or check is used for speed and easy scanning. (This is used by instructors and coaches in many fields.) There is a small space for notes which could also be used to mark choices for semi-finalists and finalists.

Practice using the scorecard at home. You may wish to refer to the chapters in this book on handling skills. Notice that the order of categories is coordinated with the judging procedure which follows.

Now Judge

Your class is in the ring. Your scorecard is in your pocket. Give clear verbal directions which can be heard by all competitors. Instruct the class to gait the dogs once around the ring at a moderate speed and stop, leaving plenty of space between dogs. Keep the class in catalog order instead of sorting large dogs and small dogs for gaiting around the ring. The importance of this first exercise is minor. It is difficult to observe numbers of dogs of such varying sizes and speeds.

Organize

Signal the class to stop and make sure each Junior has handling space. If the Juniors cannot be spaced along one side of the ring, split the class and use both sides of the ring. Leave the end of the ring empty for individual gaiting and turns. Scan the ring to make sure all Juniors have control over their dogs.

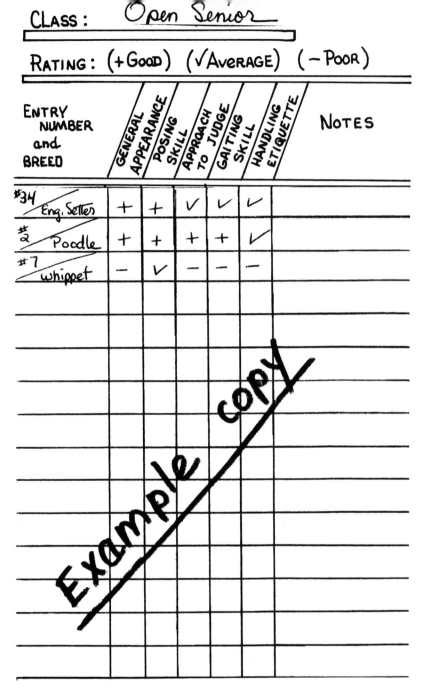

CLASS: Open Senior

RATING: (+Good) (√Average) (−Poor)

ENTRY NUMBER and BREED	GENERAL APPEARANCE	POSING SKILL	APPROACH TO JUDGE	GAITING SKILL	HANDLING ETIQUETTE	NOTES
#34 Eng. Setter	+	+	√	√	√	
#2 Poodle	+	+	+	+	√	
#7 Whippet	−	√	−	−	−	

Sample sheet from the JS Judge's Scorecard designed and copyrighted © 1978 by the authors of this book. Padded "Hallscored" cards may be obtained from the authors by writing them care of Howell Book House, 230 Park Avenue, New York, N.Y. 10017.

Examine

Using the following procedure, examine each Junior's ability.
   Call out the Junior for posed examination.
   Request gaiting in a straight down and back pattern.
   Send the Junior back to place.
Mark your scoresheet after each part of the examination. You
will have time to mark the fifth category, Handling Etiquette,
while the next Junior is getting ready.

There are several reasons for this procedure. Each Junior
has proper space to pose the dog and the judge has room for
examination. The I pattern takes the least time and is sufficient
for the basic gaiting test. You can immediately determine how
far along you are in judging the class when Juniors return to
the same place. This also eliminates the continued moving up
in line which is awkward and tiring.

A JS judge need not physically examine the posed dogs in a
class. However, you must be consistent. If you examine one
dog in a class you should examine all.

Sort

When you have examined and gaited all the Juniors in the
class, look back over the class carefully. Compare your scoresheet with your proposed choices. If the class is large, decide
on an appropriate number of competitors to "pull out." Try to
limit your semi-final choices to four, six or no more than eight.
If you bring out only four do not excuse the rest of the class; if
a Junior becomes ill and must leave the ring, there would be
no one for fourth place.

Be precise when you select your semi-finalists. Call each one
out and direct each Junior to a particular place in the ring.
Mark the semi-finalists on the scoresheet. Look back once
more over the remaining entries to check your decision. If you
have chosen more than four semi-finalists, you may ask the
steward to dismiss the rest of the class.

Re-examine

Now re-examine the Juniors in the ring. You may choose to request a different gaiting pattern either individually, in pairs or in a group. In very close competition you may even ask a question such as, "What country did your breed come from?" or "Point to the occiput."

Decide

Arrange the Juniors in the order of your choice. Announce the placement to each finalist. Direct them to the ring markers. Mark your judge's book with numbers only. Give out the ribbons and awards. Have the steward send the winners to the judge's table. Record in the judge's book the necessary information and sign the bottom.

Minor changes in this judging procedure may be necessary under certain conditions. In very small classes semi-finalists are not chosen. In very large classes it is wise to instruct half the class to relax their dogs while you are judging the other half. In extreme heat you may choose to have all Juniors relax their dogs while they are waiting for the initial examination. (On one occasion a JS judge allowed juniors to work in extremely humid weather until one girl fainted.)

Remember, your job is to test and select the best handlers. Junior Showmanship is not a performance nor entertainment.

Comment

You may wish to have the steward tell each Junior that you will be available for comments after all the classes are judged. Your scorecard is a must here. Talk to Juniors individually. Don't discuss any Junior's mistake in front of others. Sometimes parents are more interested in comments than their children. Your conversation, however, must be directed toward the Junior—with parents invited. Always begin with positive comments. If a Junior asks you to make a note of skills to practice or other information, write it on the plain side of the armband.

Special Tips

Give simple, clear directions.

Be patient—especially with first time handlers.

Pull a Junior out of line to move ahead but never move a junior back.

Don't have Juniors switch places to change ability order.

Have the steward thank each Junior for entering (at the class finish).

Know if there is a bitch in season in the ring. Place dog and handler last in line or among bitches.

Don't gait dogs toward the exit or toward other dogs.

Don't choose your winners while they are gaiting unless the four are in order.

JUNIOR SHOWMANSHIP RECORD

Date	Show and Place	Dog's Name	Award	Remarks

Suggestion: If more space is needed, Xerox copies of this page, or use it as a model in drawing your own record forms.